DISCARDED

Colombia

A Study of the Educational System of Colombia and a Guide to the Academic Placement of Students from Colombia in Educational Institutions of the United States

AP 1 '91

Stanley Wellington, Ph.D.

International Credentials Evaluator
George Mason University

1984

A Service of the International Education Activities
American Association of Collegiate Registrars and Adr

D1286081

Placement Recommendations Approved
by the National Council on the Evaluation
of Foreign Educational Credentials

Library of Congress Cataloging in Publication Data

Wellington, Stanley.
   Colombia, a study of the educational system of Colombia and a guide to the academic placement of students from Colombia in educational institutions in the United States.

   (World education series)
   Bibliography: p.
   Includes index.
   1. Education—Colombia. 2. School management and organization—Colombia. 3. Universities and colleges—Colombia—Directories. 4. School grade placement—United States. 5. School credits—United States. 6. College credits—United States. I. Title. II. Series.
LA566.W45   1984   370'.9861   84-6444
ISBN 0-910054-80-0

Publication of the World Education Series is funded by grants from the Directorate for Educational and Cultural Affairs of the United States Information Agency.

Contents

Tables

Documents

Preface

Writing this book has been a challenge and a privilege. Contrast characterizes Colombian education as it does all other aspects of Colombian society. I trust, therefore, that anything in this volume that deviates from readers' impressions of Colombian education may be explained by the discrepancy between that which is generally reported and that which actually occurs. At the same time, I take full responsibility for any errors that may appear in the following pages.

Many dedicated educators in the United States and Colombia contributed to the development of this volume, and working with them has been an enriching experience. To Joseph P. Capobianco, author of the World Education Series (WES) volume, *Italy*, who has been a painstaking but delightful monitor, I am deeply grateful for his skillful guidance. I owe a similar debt to Lucy McDermott, WES managing editor, and her assistant, Henrianne Wakefield. I am also grateful to the following persons for their advice, assistance and support: Karlene N. Dickey, Alton S. Donnelly, James S. Frey, G. James Haas, Gary Hoover, Alan Margolis, M. Mobin Shorish, and Kitty M. Villa.

In Colombia I want to thank the many educators who gave generously of their time in interviews, preparing research material, responding to enquiries, and reviewing sections of the draft. I especially wish to express my sincere thanks to Dr. Jairo Caicedo C., Jefe Relaciones Internacionales, Instituto Colombiano para el Fomento de la Educación Superior; Dr. Margoth Supúlveda Niño; Dr. Pedro Polo U., Decano Académico, Pontificia Universidad Javeriana; Dr. Francisco Genecco-Calvo, Fulbright Commission; Dr. Luis Alberto Maldonado S., Director del Departamento de Admisiones e Información Profesional, Universidad Nacional de Colombia; Director Fernando Villegas-Angel, Secretariado Permanente del Episcopado Colombiano; Dr. Rodolfo Uribe Uribe; Ing. Hortensio Castro O.; Sra. María de las Angeles Chamorro; Prof. Myriam Murillo Gasper; and Srta. Laura Olga Montoya Montero. Their spirit of cooperation truly indicated their deep concern for Colombian education.

At my own institution I wish to express special appreciation to France J. Pruitt, Director of International Programs and Services at George Mason University, who encouraged this assignment and gave unqualified support throughout the production of the book. Other members of the George Mason community to whom I would like to express my gratitude include Ali-Asghar Aghbar, José Angel Bufill, Martha S. Daza and Hamdesa Tuso.

Finally, I wish to thank my wife, Simin S. Wellington, for her patience and assistance throughout this project.

COLOMBIA

Chapter One

Introduction and Primary Education

Official Name: República de Colombia (Republic of Colombia).

Location and Size: 439,737 square miles (1,138,914 sq. km.), located on the northwest corner of South America. Colombia is bordered on the north by the Caribbean Sea, on the east by Venezuela and Brazil, on the south by Brazil, Perú, and Ecuador, and the west by Ecuador, the Pacific Ocean, Panamá, and the Caribbean.

Government: Democracy.

Legislative Body: Congress (bicameral), consisting of a Senate and a Chamber of Representatives. The Senate has 112 members, the Chamber 199 members.

Local Government: 22 departments, the Distrito Especial/D.E. (Special District) of Bogotá, 3 *intendencias* and 5 *comisarías*, under appointed governors and administrators.[1]

Population: 28,776,000 (1980 est.)

Main Ethnic Groups: 60% mixed European and Indian descent, 20% Caucasian, 14% mulatto, 4% African, and 2% Indian.

Language: Spanish is the official language.

Religion: Over 95% of the population is Roman Catholic.

Largest Cities: The estimated populations of the four largest cities were as follows in 1979: Bogotá, capital, 4,324,000; Medellín, 1,589,000; Cali, 1,382,000; Barranquilla, 891,000.

Leading Industries: Agriculture (bananas, cassava, cattle, coffee, corn, cotton, potatoes, wheat); mining (coal, emeralds, gold, iron, natural gas, oil, platinum, silver); manufacturing (chemicals, steel, textiles).

SOURCE: *Hammond Almanac*, 14th ed., s.v. "Colombia"; and *Concise Columbia Encyclopedia*, 1983 ed., s.v. "Colombia."

1. *Intendencias* and *comisarías* (subdelegations) are political subdivisions that do not qualify as states because of low population density.

Table 1.1. **Chart of the Colombian Educational System, 1983**

	Preschool	Primary	Basic Sec. Cycle	Advanced Sec. Cycle	Higher Education	Graduate Education
Years of Colombian Education	[ ]-[ ]-[ ]	1 2 3 4 5 [1]-[2]-[3]-[4]-[5] C	6 7 8 9 [1]-[2]-[3]-[4]	10 11	12 13 14 15 16 17 18	

Advanced Sec. Cycle

Academic/Classical [5] - [6] B
Arts* [5] - [6] B
Commercial [5] - [6] B
Gen. Agriculture [5] - [6] B
Industrial [5] - [6] B
Pedagogy/Teacher Training [5] - [6] B
Social Studies [5] - [6] B
Ages: 16 17

Higher Education

Formación Intermedia Profesional
Level 1
[1]-[2] TPI

Formación Tecnológica
Level 2
[1]-[2]-[3] - [1]-[2] T TS

Formación Universitaria
Level 3
[1]-[2]-[3]-[4]- [5]- [6]- [7] L L M I I MC
Ages: 18 19 20 21 22 23 24

Graduate Education

Formación Avanzada o de Postgrado
Level 4
[1]-[2]- [3]-[4] E E E
[1]-[2]- [3]-[4] MA D

KEY:
C — Certificado al Quinto Grado de Enseñanza Primaria
B — Bachiller diploma
TPI — Técnico Profesional Intermedio (4-5 sem. program)
T — Tecnólogo (4-7 sem. program)
TS — Tecnólogo Especializado; program approved and scheduled to begin functioning in 1984
L — Licenciado or comparable first university degree
I — Ingeniero degree
M — Médico degree
MC — Médico Cirujano degree
E — Especialista
MA — Magister degree
D — Doctor degree
* — Experimental program since 1978

Ages   4 5 6   7 8 9 10 11   12 13 14 15

Brief Overview of the Educational Structure

The Ministerio de Educación Nacional (Ministry of National Education) is the major administrative authority in Colombia for all levels of education. The Ministry exercises control over public and private (both secular and parochial) schools, including the large and influential school system of the Roman Catholic Church except for those institutions engaged in the training of religious personnel. This authority extends from the President to the Minister of Education and through him to the *departamentos* (states), the *municipios* (municipal districts), and the decentralized institutes such as the Instituto Colombiano para el Fomento de la Educación Superior/ICFES (Colombian Institute for the Promotion of Higher Education).

Each of the 23 states in the country, and Bogotá, the Distrito Especial/D.E. (special district), has a *Secretario de Educación* (Secretary of Education). The Secretaries of Education, who are appointed by the Governor of each state, administer education in their jurisdictions in accordance with the standards established by the Ministry.

The state legislatures are responsible for establishing new schools under their jurisdictions and for providing funding to enable them to function properly. In every other aspect, the educational system is the responsibility of the Ministry of National Education. This includes the determination of types of curriculums, minimum course requirements, the school calendar (except for university-level institutions), qualifications for teachers, etc. The Ministry also inspects all public and private schools for compliance with national laws and decrees.

The School Calendar

There are two school calendars in Colombia, designated Calendars A and B. Calendar A is used by most of the country. The area where Calendar B is used includes the *departamentos* (states) of Valle, Cauca, and Nariño, and the *Comisaría* of Putumayo.[2]

Institutions at every level from primary through higher non-university education operate on one of these two calendars which, like most other aspects of education, are mandated by the Ministry of National Education. The primary and secondary schools are in session five days a week (Monday through Friday), 198 days a year. Both calendars allow a week's vacation at Easter in addition to the regular vacation periods cited below. The calendars are as follows:

Calendar A: The first semester begins February 1 and ends June 15, with a vacation period from June 16 to July 15. The second semester begins July 16 and ends November 30, with vacation during December and January.

---

2. Decree 1902 of 1969.

Calendar B: The first semester begins September 1 and ends December 15, with vacation from that date until January 15. The second semester begins January 15 and ends June 30, with vacation during July and August.

Frequency of Reform

During the past century, Colombia has experienced almost constant reform of its educational system. This has been particularly true during the past thirty years, as the demand for education at all social and economic levels has steadily increased.

As with most aspects of education in Colombia, reform is the responsibility of the Ministry of National Education. The Ministry has the power to issue *decretos* (decrees) and *resoluciones* (resolutions), which are the legal foundation of the educational structure. Thus, it will be noted throughout this volume that every educational function operates under an official governmental decree or resolution. Also, it will be noted that certain aspects of one level of education may be operating under a decree or resolution different from that of another aspect, a symptom of the frequent and overlapping reforms, some of which are allowed to lapse into disuse.

In fact, despite the various reforms, the basic structure remains unchanged, especially in primary and secondary education. But if the structure is unchanged, there is evidence of progress in elements of the system. At the secondary level it consists of a broader curriculum. At the higher education level, it is reflected in the greater stress placed upon the importance of technological education. Also, more graduate programs are being implemented.

For more information on the most recent reform of secondary education, see Appendix B and Chapter Two. For a discussion of higher education, see Chapter Three.

Preschool and Primary Education

Children may enter kindergarten (*jardín infantil*) as early as age 4 and continue through age 6. Most kindergartens are private in Colombia.

The majority of the primary schools are free public institutions operated by the state governments with assistance from the Ministry of National Education. Most private schools are Roman Catholic. Children may enter the five-year public primary schools at age 6, although most enter at 7.

Self-contained classrooms are the rule. Ordinarily, teachers spend approximately 6 hours a day, made up of two sessions, with their students. Each session consists of three 45-minute class periods with a 45-minute break between the two sessions. In a situation where a school is overcrowded and it is necessary to have two shifts, the school day is divided into two parts. The students will still attend six class periods of 45 minutes each. The first of such shifts often begins at 6:50 A.M. and ends at 12:40 P.M.; the second begins at

12:50 and ends at 6:35 P.M. Double shifts are not unusual in many areas of Colombia. At the end of the first term, partial examinations are conducted; final examinations are held upon completion of the second term. Students passing all subjects move on to the next grade without additional requirements. Those who fail in one or two subjects are required to pass subsequent examinations in order to qualify in those subjects before they can be promoted to the next grade. Students who fail three or more subjects must repeat the grade level.

The primary school curriculum, including the number of subjects at each grade level, time spent on each subject, and the topics to be covered, is specified in detail by the Ministry of National Education. See Table 1.2 for the current primary school curriculum.

Table 1.2. **Primary School Curriculum, by Grade**

		Hours per Week			
Subjects	Grade: 1	2	3	4	5
Aesthetic and Manual Training	3	3	3	3	3
Mathematics	5	5	5	5	5
Natural Science	3	3	4	4	5
Physical Education	3	3	3	3	3
Religious and Moral Training	3	3	3	3	3
Social Studies	4	4	5	5	5
Spanish	9	9	7	7	6
Totals	30	30	30	30	30

SOURCE: Decree 1710 of 1963, and Resolution 2308 of 1971.

The grading system in primary schools is on a scale of 1 to 5, with 3 as the lowest passing grade. These grades are sometimes written as 10 to 50, or in *letras* (descriptive terms). For example, see Document 1, a *Certificado al Quinto Grado de Enseñanza Primaria* (certificate of completion of grade 5), the last year of primary school. Document 1 shows the fifth year *área* (subjects); *intensidad horaria* (hours per week); *promedio número* (final average grade in numbers); and *promedio letras* (final average grade in descriptive terms). The certificate of completion of grade 5 is the sole requirement for entrance to secondary school.

ALCALDIA MAYOR DE BOGOTA
SECRETARIA DE EDUCACION
DIVISION DE PRIMARIA

CERTIFICADO

Los suscritos, Director (a) y Profesor (a) del grado quinto de la Concentración Distrital

_____ Britalia _____ Zona 8D

Certifican que el alumno (a) _____

curso y aprobó durante el año lectivo de 1978 los estudios correspondientes al Quinto Grado
de Enseñanza Primaria con las siguientes calificaciones e intensidad horaria:

A R E A	Intensidad Horaria	Promedio Numeros	Premedio Letras
Educacion religiosa y moral	3	40	cuatro cero
Matemáticas	5	35	tres cinco
Lenguaje	6	45	cuatro cinco
Estudios Sociales	5	40	cuatro cero
Ciencias naturales	5	45	cuatro cinco
Educación estética y manual	3	40	cuatro cero
Educación física	3	45	cuatro cinco
Conducta		50	cinco cero

Expedido en Bogotá, D.E., a los (26)   días del mes de Noviembre _____ de 1978

Director,

___Felio F. Rodriguez C._____

Nombres.   Apellidos   Profesor,

_____   _____
Firma - c.c.: 19169257 de Bta   Firma / c.c.: 4242450
                                                    Santa Rosa De V

Nota: Las firmas de este certificado no necesitan ser autenticadas según Decreto Nacional
Número 3503 de Diciembre 28 de 1962 del Ministerio de Educación.

No. 1. *Certificado al Quinto Grado de Enseñanza Primaria* (Certificate of Completion of Grade 5).

Chapter Two

Secondary and Non-Formal Education

Secondary Education

There are two terms used to refer to secondary education in Colombia. The most familiar is *educación media* (middle education); the other is *educación secundaria* (secondary education). Both terms refer to years VI through XI of Colombian secondary school education. In this volume, the term "secondary education" will be used to refer to all education which follows primary school and precedes higher education. Secondary school is six years in length.

Students enter secondary school directly upon successful completion of five years of primary school, usually at age 12. The certificate of completion of grade 5 is the sole requirement for admission to public secondary schools. Most private schools administer their own entrance examination, upon which admission and placement is based.

The secondary schools are generally called *colegios* ("colleges"), although the terms *liceo* or *instituto* may be used as well, particularly by private schools. Included among the public schools are the *Institutos Nacionales de Enseñanza Media Diversificada*/INEM (literally, national institutions of diversified education; commonly called "comprehensive secondary schools"). Because the INEM system was established in 1969, these schools are discussed in the section on secondary education prior to 1974. They are, however, an important part of the current public secondary system.

The six-year programs of secondary schools represent the traditional route to university education in Colombia. Most private secondary schools offer a curriculum that emphasizes the *Bachiller Académico o Clásico* (academic or classical secondary school diploma), although since 1974 under Decree 080 all secondary schools by law are required to offer at least one other curriculum besides that leading to the academic diploma. The public secondary schools, which in general serve the lower income strata of the population, offer a more diverse curriculum that leads to all types of higher education, or to employment. Although the *Bachiller* (of any type) is considered the basic requirement for entrance to institutions of higher education in Colombia, applicants must also pass the official entrance examination, *El Examen de Estado* (The State Examination) in order to be accepted. See Chapter Three for a discussion of this exam.

7

Secondary Curriculums

Current Curriculums

Although the educational system has been reformed frequently during the last century, the basic structure of secondary education remains much the same: a four-year cycle followed by a two-year cycle. Upon completion of the second cycle, the student receives a diploma, the *Bachiller* (the term may be used as the designation for a diploma or for a person who has received such a diploma). The legal and practical value of the *Bachiller* remains the same as before the most recent reforms.

All of the secondary programs that lead to a *Bachiller* are called *Bachillerato* programs. Since January 22, 1974, secondary education in Colombia has been operating on the following two cycles: 1) *Ciclo Básico* (basic cycle; also called "basic common cycle"), the first four years of secondary school or *Bachillerato* years VI through IX; and 2) *Ciclo Vocacional* (literally, vocational cycle; also called "advanced secondary cycle"), *Bachillerato* years X and XI. Note that the term "vocational cycle" as it is used in this instance denotes the U.S. idea of "choice of career" rather than that of lower technical education.

Basic Cycle

During the first two years of the *Ciclo Básico* (basic cycle), years VI and VII, all students receive the same fundamental academic education. In addition, each student spends 5 hours per week in "vocational exploration" chosen from four areas: agricultural, commercial, industrial, and social studies education. During the last two years of the basic cycle, years VIII and IX, in addition to the four areas mentioned above, there are two other areas from which students may select a certain number of hours per week for "vocational initiation": the academic and pedagogy curriculums. See Table 2.1 for the basic cycle curriculum. This structure allows students to move easily among the vocational initiation areas.

Table 2.1. **Curriculum, *Ciclo Básico* (Basic Cycle)**

Section A: Common Academic Subjects				
		Hours per Week		
Years:	VI	VII	VIII	IX
Aesthetic Education	2	2	2	2
Foreign Languages	4	4	3	3
Mathematics	5	5	4	4
Natural Science	4	4	4	4
Physical Education	2	2	2	2
Religious Education	2	2	2	2
Social Science	6	6	4	4
Spanish Language & Literature	5	5	4	4
Subtotal	30	30	25	25

Vocational Exploration—Selected from
  the following areas: Commercial,

General Agriculture, Industrial, Social
Studies

	Years:	VIII	IX		
		5	5	*	*
Totals		35	35	35-38	35-38

Section B: Vocational Initiation Curriculum by Areas—Years VIII, IX

		Hours per Week	
Areas	Years:	VIII	IX
Academic†			
Second Foreign Language		5	5
Electives:			
Health Education (Human Anatomy/			
Physiology)		—	5
Vocational Workshop		5	—
	Totals	10	10
Commercial			
Accounting		—	5
Stenography		4	3
Typing		6	2
	Totals	10	10
General Agriculture			
Agricultural Exploration		4	4
Animal Science		4	4
Rural Construction		2	2
	Totals	10	10
Industrial			
Electricity		—	5
Metal Mechanics		—	5
Technical Drawing		5	—
Wood Construction		5	—
	Totals	10	10
Pedagogy†			
Agricultural Techniques or Crafts		2	—
Methods & Techniques of Teaching		2	2
Observation of Student Teaching		3	—
Sociology of Education & Community			
Project		—	3
Student Teaching		—	3
Techniques & Foundations of Educa-			
tion		4	4
Workshop of Educational Skills		2	—
	Totals	13	12
Social Studies			
Basic Studies of Administration		—	2
Communication Techniques		—	4
Community Development		4	—
Dressmaking & Sewing		—	4
Human Biology & Health		6	4
	Totals	10	14

SOURCE: Resolution 130, January 23, 1978, and Resolution 4785, July 9, 1974.

*Depending upon area selected. See Section B of this table.

†During the last two years of the basic cycle, the academic and pedagogy curriculums are added to the other four to increase the areas offered for vocational initiation to six, as opposed to four for vocational exploration.

Advanced Secondary Cycle

The *Ciclo Vocacional* (literally, vocational cycle; more aptly translated "advanced secondary cycle"; sometimes called *Ensenānza Media Diversificada*, as in Document 2.7) consists of the last two years of secondary school, years X and XI. Currently, it is considered a two-year specialization program, although of the various programs offered the *Bachillerato Académico o Clásico* (academic or classical program) remains the standard. Appendix B describes proposed reforms of Decree 1419 of 1978, which is still in the planning stage and for which as yet only one curriculum, the *Bachillerato en Artes*, has been developed.

The secondary programs currently offered are listed below. All of the programs require 35 class hours per week, except pedagogy, which requires 39, and all of the programs lead to the *Bachiller* (diploma) in the specialization studied. The curriculums for all of the current programs are shown in Tables 2.2–2.7. The programs are as follows:

1. *Bachillerato Académico o Clásico* (secondary program of academic or classical education; popularly called "general secondary education"). The two programs are identical, except that a classical *Bachillerato* program will almost always offer Latin as a second language, and students in the program will be

Table 2.2. **Curriculum, *Bachillerato Académico o Clásico*, *Ciclo Vocacional***
(Academic or Classical Education, Advanced Secondary Cycle)/
Two Specializations

Science Specialization			Humanities Specialization		
Subjects	hpw		Subjects	hpw	
Years	X	XI	Years	X	XI
Aesthetic Education	2	—	Aesthetic Education	2	—
Biology	5	4	Art	—	4
Earth Science	—	3	Economics	4	—
Foreign Languages	2	2	Economic, Social &		
General Chemistry	6	—	Political Institutions		
Mathematics	6	6	of 20th Cent.	4	—
Organic Chemistry	—	4	Foreign Languages	3	3
Philosphy	2	2	Foreign Language (2nd)	4	4
Physical Education	2	2	Intro. to Psych. &		
Physics	5	5	Sociology	—	4
Religious Education	2	2	Language & Lit. Wkshp.	4	4
Social Science	—	2	Mathematics	3	3
Spanish & Literature	3	3	Natural Science	—	2
Totals	35	35	Philosophy	2	2
			Physical Education	2	2
			Religious Education	2	2
			Social Science	2	2
			Spanish & Literature	3	3
			Totals	35	35

SOURCE: Resolution 130, January 23, 1978.

encouraged to take it. Note that one type of institution, the minor seminaries of the Roman Catholic Church, almost always grants the *Bachiller Clásico*. The minor seminaries are secondary-level institutions, regulated by the Ministry of National Education, with the same program as that offered by the general secondary schools. Graduates may apply to any institution of higher education including the major seminaries. Seminary education is discussed in Appendix D.

2. *Bachillerato Pedagógico* or *Formación Normalista* (secondary program in pedagogy or teacher training). These are identical programs.

3. *Bachillerato Industrial* (secondary program of industrial education).

4. *Bachillerato Comercial* (secondary program of commercial education).

5. *Bachillerato Agropecuario* (secondary program in general agriculture).

6. *Bachillerato en Promoción Social* (secondary program in social studies).

7. *Bachillerato en Artes* (secondary program in the arts). Experimental program (since 1978); offered in only two schools at present. See Appendix B for a discussion of Decree 1419, and Appendix C for the arts curriculum.

Table 2.3. **Curriculum, *Bachillerato Pedagógico* or *Formación Normalista*, *Ciclo Vocacional* (Pedagogical or Teacher Training, Advanced Secondary Cycle)**

Subjects	hpw		Subjects	hpw	
Years	X	XI	Years	X	XI
Aesthetic Educ. (Music, Dance, Theater)	2	2	History & Philosophy of Education	3	3
Aesthetic, Moral & Religious Educ.	1	1	Mathematics	3	3
Anthropology	—	2	Methodology of Teaching	2	1
Behavior & Health	2	2	Physical Education	2	2
Chemistry	3	3	Physics	3	3
Educational Administration	2	—	Sociology of Education	—	4
Educational Psychology	3	—	Spanish	4	4
Foreign Language (elec.)	3	3	Student Teaching	6	6
			Totals	39	39

SOURCE: Resolution 4785, July 9, 1974.

Table 2.4. **Curriculum, *Bachillerato Industrial*, *Ciclo Vocacional* (Industrial Education, Advanced Secondary Cycle)/Four Specializations**

Core Curriculum Common to all Four Specializations		
Subjects	hpw	
Year	X	XI
Foreign Languages	2	2
Philosophy	2	2

(continued)

	X	XI
Physical Education	2	2
Religious Education	2	2
Spanish & Literature	3	3

Construction Specialization

Subjects	hpw	
Years	X	XI
Architectural Drawing	5	5
Mathematics	3	3
Physics	3	3
Social Science	2	2
Theory	4	4
Workshop	7	7
Totals	35	35

Electricity and Electronics Specialization

Subjects	hpw	
Years	X	XI
Aesthetic Education	2	—
Electric & Electronic Drawing	3	3
Electronic & Electric Theory	3	3
Electronic & Electric Wkshp.	10	10
Mathematics	3	3
Physics	3	3
Social Science	—	2
Totals	35	35

Industrial Chemistry Specialization

Subjects	hpw	
Years	X	XI
Chemical Analysis	—	5
General Chemistry	6	—
Industrial Chemistry	5	4
Mathematics	6	3
Organic Chemistry	—	5
Physics	5	5
Social Science	2	2
Totals	35	35

Metal Mechanics Specialization

Subjects	hpw	
Years	X	XI
Aesthetic Education	2	—
Mathematics	3	3
Metal Mechanics Wkshp.	10	10
Physics	3	3
Social Science	—	2
Technical-Mechanical Drawing	3	3
Theory of Metal Mechanics	3	3
Totals	35	35

SOURCE: Resolution 130, January 23, 1978.

Table 2.5. **Curriculum, *Bachillerato Comercial, Ciclo Vocacional* (Commercial Education, Advanced Secondary Cycle)/Two Specializations**

Core Curriculum Common to Both Specializations					
Subjects	hpw		Subjects	hpw	
Years	X	XI	Years	X	XI
Foreign Languages	2	2	Physical Education	2	2
Mathematics	3	3	Religious Education	2	2
Natural Science	3	3	Spanish & Literature	3	3

Accounting Specialization

Subjects	hpw	
Years	X	XI
Accounting	5	5
Aesthetic Education	2	—
Business Law	5	—
Commercial Practice	—	6
Economics	4	—
Office Management	2	—
Philosophy	2	2
Social Science	—	2
Statistics	—	5
Totals	35	35

Secretarial Specialization

Subjects	hpw	
Years	X	XI
Accounting	3	—
Aesthetic Education	2	2
Commercial English	—	2
Commercial Practice	—	6
Editing	2	—
Law	3	—
Office Management	5	—
Social Science	2	2
Statistics	—	3
Stenography	3	—
Typing	—	5
Totals	35	35

SOURCE: Resolution 130, January 23, 1978.

Table 2.6. **Curriculum,** *Bachillerato Agropecuario, Ciclo Vocacional*
(General Agriculture, Advanced Secondary Cycle)

Subjects	hpw		Subjects	hpw	
Years	X	XI	Years	X	XI
Aesthetic Education	2	2	Philosophy	2	2
Agricultural Exploration	5	5	Physical Education	2	2
Animal Sci. Exploration	5	5	Religious Education	2	2
Foreign Languages	2	2	Rural Construction	3	3
Mathematics	3	3	Rural Devel. Programs	3	3
Natural Science	3	3	Spanish & Literature	3	3
			Totals	35	35

SOURCE: Resolution 130, January 23, 1978.

Table 2.7. **Curriculum,** *Bachillerato Promoción Social, Ciclo Vocacional*
(Social Studies Education, Advanced Secondary Cycle)

Subjects	hpw		Subjects	hpw	
Years	X	XI	Years	X	XI
Aesthetic Education	2	1	Natural Science	3	3
Adult Education	—	3	Nutrition	3	3
Education for Community Devel.	5	—	Philosophy	2	2
Field Practice	—	8	Physical Education	2	2
Foreign Languages	2	2	Recreation	3	—
Health Education	—	3	Social Science	2	2
Intro. to Psych. & Sociology	5	—	Spanish & Literature	3	3
Mathematics	3	3	Totals	35	35

SOURCE: Resolution 130, January 23, 1978.

Curriculums Prior to 1974

Secondary education in Colombia prior to 1974 was offered through four curriculums. The program consisted of a four-year *Ciclo Básico* (basic cycle), years VI-IX, followed by a two-year *Ciclo Segundo* (second cycle), years X-XI. Although the terminology has changed slightly, the system was basically the same as the current system. The curriculums offered were the following:

1. *Bachillerato Académico o Clásico* (academic or classical secondary program; popularly called "general secondary education").

2. *Normal* education (teacher training).

3. Vocational or technical education.

4. The *Institutos Nacionales de Enseñanza Media Diversificada*/INEM (the "diversified secondary schools"). These schools are also part of the current system.

Academic or Classical Program. The academic program, then as now, prepared students to enter a university or other institutions of higher education. Students who satisfactorily completed the second cycle received the diploma *Bachiller Académico o Clásico*, which admitted them to all Colombian institutions of higher education upon successful completion of an entrance exam. (See Documents 2.1 and 2.2 and their description under "Documents— Current and Pre-1974.")

Normal Education. The purpose of *normal* education was to train students as elementary school teachers. The curriculum for the basic cycle was the same as that of the academic *Bachillerato* program. The second cycle involved specialization and was made up of four five-month periods called *quimester*. The diploma or title, called either *Maestro(a)*, *Maestro(a) Superior*, or *Normalista Superior* (all meaning "teacher"), qualified these secondary school graduates to teach in elementary schools and allowed them to apply for entrance to Colombian institutions of higher education. Acceptance to these institutions, however, was dependent upon successful completion of the entrance exam.

Vocational or Technical Education. This curriculum included three specializations—commercial, industrial, and agricultural—all discussed below.

- Commercial Education. Commercial education on the secondary level was designed to teach business techniques that would allow students to undertake administrative activities at intermediate levels in banking, business, industry, and public administration.

  A student who finished the four-year basic cycle of the secondary commercial curriculum (nine years of education) and who worked one year in a business which attested to the student's efficiency was granted the diploma or title of *Experto* (expert).

  The second cycle, years X-XI, required two additional years of commercial studies. The *Bachiller Técnico Comercial* (commercial technical diploma) was conferred upon successful completion of the second cycle. Holders of this diploma could apply for admission to any Colombian institution of higher education. To be accepted, however, it was also necessary to pass an entrance exam (see Chapter Three for a discussion of higher education entrance exams.).

- Industrial Education. The objective of industrial education, which was offered in schools called *Institutos Técnicos Industriales* (technical industrial institutes), was to provide students with the necessary skills to work effectively in industry. This program included specializations such as cabinetwork, drafting, electricity, foundry work, mechanics, shoemaking, tailoring, etc.

The diploma *Experto* was granted upon completion of the first cycle of four years' length (a total of nine years of education). See Document 2.5.

The length of the second cycle of industrial education was changed from two years to three years in 1966 by Decree 718. This change meant that the *Bachiller Técnico Industrial* (technical industrial diploma) was granted at the end of a total of 12 years of education. Students holding such a diploma were eligible to apply for admission to all Colombian institutions of higher education. However, in order to be admitted, they had to pass an entrance exam. (See Chapter Three for a discussion of higher education entrance exams.)

● Agricultural Education. The first cycle of secondary education in general agriculture was offered in *Escuelas Vocacionales Agrícolas* (vocational schools of agriculture). Located in the rural regions, these schools offered a four-year basic cycle that was essentially the same as that for the academic or classical program, but which also included some technical subjects such as cattle breeding and dairy operation.

The second cycle, which was lengthened from two to three years in 1966 by Decree 718, was offered in *Institutos Técnicos Agropecuarios* (technical schools of general agriculture). Admission to the second cycle was based upon completion of the basic cycle. The three-year second cycle curriculum integrated academic or classical education subjects with agricultural subjects, including animal science and the cultivation of crops. The *Bachiller Técnico Agrícola* (technical agricultural diploma), awarded for successful completion of the secondary program and representing 12 years of study, qualified the student to apply for admission to all Colombian institutions of higher education. An entrance exam was also required. (See Chapter Three for a discussion of entrance exams for institutions of higher education.)

The INEM System. The *Institutos Nacionales de Enseñanza Media Diversificada* (literally, national institutes of diversified education, but generally translated as "comprehensive secondary schools") introduced a new concept in curriculums to Colombia. Although the plan of studies at INEM institutions has undergone various changes since the inception of the system as an experiment in 1969, the institutes now operate under Resolution 130 of 1978 that established the current curriculum for the public and private secondary schools. This means that the schools operate on the four-year *Ciclo Básico* (basic cycle) and the two-year *Ciclo Vocacional* (advanced secondary cycle) leading to the *Bachiller*. The curriculum offered is the same as that of the current system and is shown in Tables 2.2-2.7. See Document 2.7 for a *Bachiller* issued by an INEM and the section on "Documents—Current and Pre-1974" for a description of the document.

When the INEM system was established as a pilot project in 1969, the Ministry of National Education defined the new type of school as an institute under a unified administration offering an academic program and various vocational programs.[1] Prior to that time, a variety of subject areas had existed

---

1. Ministerio de Educación Nacional, *Política Educativa Nacional. Serie del Educador No. 2* (Bogotá: Ministerio de Educación Nacional, 1975), p. 108.

at the secondary level, but each had been administered and directed at a separate type of school. The INEM schools concentrated all of the different specializations (*modalidades*) under one establishment. Many of the ideas embodied in the curriculum introduced in Resolution 130 of 1978 were derived from the experimental curriculum of the INEM system.

The comprehensive secondary schools are highly regarded in Colombia because of their excellent facilities and high salary standard for teachers. The first of the INEM schools were opened in 1970, one in each of the following cities: Bogotá, Medellín, Cali, Bucaramanga, Barranquilla, Cúcuta, Pasto, and Santa Marta. Since that time approximately a dozen more have been opened in cities all over Colombia. Half of the cost of the INEM system was borne by the International Bank of Reconstruction and Development, and half by the Colombian government. Assistance in training personnel has been provided by the United States Agency for International Development.

Grading at the Secondary Level

Current System

Since 1974, secondary school grades have been awarded on a scale of 1 to 10 (highest), with 6 as the lowest passing grade. Grades of 10 are rare, and an overall average of 10 is nonexistent. This would suggest that 10 is an A +, and that 9 is a very good grade indeed.

As with all comparisons of grading systems between different cultures, equating the two accurately is extremely difficult, if not impossible. The use of the suggested grade equivalencies between Colombian secondary schools and U.S. high schools offered here should be tempered with judgement.

Admissions officers should also be aware that Colombian grades typically are reported as whole numbers with decimal subdivisions in tenths, e.g., 8 (*ocho*), 8.0 (*ocho-cero*), 80 (*ochenta*), 8.4 (*ocho-cuatro*), 84 (*ochenta y cuatro*). Grades with decimal subdivisions represent quality in between two whole numbers and this should be taken into account when transcripts are being evaluated.

Because the concept of a D grade, i.e., a passing but unsatisfactory grade, does not exist in the Colombian system, a D equivalent has not been included in the suggested grade equivalencies in Tables 2.8 and 2.9.

Under the current system, it is required that all grades in *Bachillerato* programs be entered on transcripts as yearly grades. One-semester courses, of course, are excluded from this regulation. The yearly grade is based on the average of the two semester grades, which are determined as follows: 1st quarter, 40%; 2nd quarter, 40%; final exam at end of semester, 20%. See Documents 2.8 and 2.9 in the section "Documents—Current and Pre-1974" for a transcript and a discussion of the grades shown. Document 2.9 is a transcript of the sixth or final year.

Report cards are issued at the end of each quarter. Numerical grades are given for each subject, along with comments from teachers.

Table 2.8. **Suggested Equivalencies Between Grading Systems of Colombian Secondary Schools and U.S. High Schools, 1974-Present**

Colombian System		U.S. Equivalent
9.5-10.0	superior (seldom attained)	A+
8.5-9.4	excellent	A
7.5-8.4	good	B
6.0-7.4	satisfactory, pass	C
1.0-5.9	fail	F

Source: Based on conversations with officials of secondary schools in Bogotá, Cali, Palmira, and Popayán.

Grading Prior to 1974

The grading system, established by Decree 1598 in 1934, was used until 1974. Based on a scale of 1 to 5 (highest), the minimum passing grade was 3. Semester grades were based on an average of the following: attendance and punctuality (15%); classwork, homework, assignments, research, and consultation (50%); participation in group activities (10%); and the exam at the end of the semester (25%). For suggested equivalence between the pre-1974 grading system and that of the United States, see Table 2.9.

Table 2.9. **Suggested Equivalencies Between Grading Systems of Colombian Secondary Schools and U.S. High Schools, 1934-74**

Colombian System	U.S. Equivalent
5 *muy bien* (very good)	A excellent/very good
4 *bien* (good)	B good
3 *regular* (satisfactory)	C satisfactory
2 *mal* (bad)	F failure
1 *muy mal* (very bad)	

Source: Based on the frequency of assigning of Colombian grades as determined in interviews with officials at secondary schools in Bogotá, Cali, Palmira, and Popayán.

Examinations and Promotion/Both Systems

Final examinations are given at the end of each semester and count approximately 20% of each semester's grade. These exams are two hours long and are given at the rate of one per day for five days. They cover only material from the preceding semester, except when the work is of a cumulative nature, as in mathematics.

The student is allowed two chances, ten days apart, to retake the final exam in any single subject in which an average grade below 6 or (60%) is received. Passing either of these second-chance exams means passing the course. Failure on both attempts means failure in the course and, at the very least, the student must repeat the subject the following year. At the most, the secondary school has the power to make the student repeat the entire year.

If a student finishes the year with grades that average out below 6 in the current system (below 3 in the old) in two subjects, one make-up exam is allowed in each subject. Passing both exams results in promotion. Passing one and failing one results in yet another make-up exam in the failed subject. Again, passing is rewarded by promotion; failure results in either repeating the failed course the following year, or repeating the entire year in all subjects.

Earning an average grade below 6 (3 in the old system) in three subjects means repeating the entire year.

Documents—Current and Pre-1974

Students who successfully complete the six-year secondary school program receive a *Bachiller* (diploma) that, along with the passing of a national entrance examination, admits them to Colombian universities or other institutions of higher education. Although there have been various reforms and changes in the educational system during the past 20 years, the *Bachiller* still represents, in most cases, the same quality and number of years of education as prior to the reform. The *Bachiller Académico o Clásico* (academic or classical secondary school diploma) has remained virtually unchanged throughout the reforms. In general, most of the changes in the educational system have involved increasing the number and types of specializations offered, and making them available to a broader spectrum of the population. The *Bachiller* diplomas offered currently and prior to 1974 are listed in Table 2.10.

The *Bachiller Académico* and the *Bachiller Pedagógico* may be earned by taking an official validation (*validación*) examination offered by the Servicio Nacional de Pruebas (National Testing Service). Offered only in these two fields, the *Bachiller* earned in this manner is, according to Decree 80, the equivalent of any other officially recognized *Bachiller*.

The *Bachiller*, as previously stated, denotes both a diploma and a person who has completed a *Bachillerato* program (secondary school). Recalling this, admissions officers will note on the sample documents shown in this section that the phrase *título de Bachiller* (title of "bachelor") appears on several of the documents. In these instances, *Bachiller* refers to the person upon whom the title was conferred.

Document 2.1 is an example of a *Bachiller Académico* from a public secondary school, and Document 2.2 is the same type of document from a private secondary school. Both documents have the seal of the Republic of Colombia and a mention of the office of the Mayor of Bogotá at the top of the page. Underneath, the name of the secondary school is given, followed by a statement that the document is issued under a certain decree or resolution of the Ministry of National Education. Both documents then state that the student has satisfactorily completed the academic curriculum and has passed all required examinations. Below are the signatures of the *Rector* (principal) of the school, and of various other officials. The only difference in the two documents is the omission of the word *académico* on Document 2.2. The document is, however, a *Bachiller Académico*, and such a format for one of

Table 2.10.   **The *Bachiller* Diplomas (Secondary School Diplomas) Offered in Colombia, Past and Present**

Bachiller (Diplomas)	Translation
Pre- and Post-1974	
Bachiller Académico/	Academic Diploma/
Bachiller Clásico	Classical Diploma*
Current Diplomas (Since 1974)	
Bachiller en Artes (since 1978)†	Diploma in Art
Bachiller Agropecuario	Diploma in General Agriculture
Bachiller Comercial	Diploma in Commercial Studies
Bachiller Industrial	Diploma in Industrial Studies
Bachiller Pedagógico	Diploma in Pedagogy
Bachiller en Promoción Social	Diploma in Social Studies
Pre-1974 Diplomas	
Bachiller Técnico Industrial	Technical Industrial Diploma
Bachiller Técnico Agrícola	Technical Agricultural Diploma
Bachiller Técnico Comercial	Technical Commercial Diploma
Maestro(a), Maestro(a) Superior, *Normalista Superior*	Primary School Teacher Diploma

*These two diplomas are considered interchangeable.

†Experimental. The first class is expected to be graduated in 1984. Two specializations are offered: *Bellas Artes* (fine arts), and *Artes Aplicada* (applied arts). See Appendix C for the curriculum.

these documents is not unusual.

Documents 2.3 and 2.4 are secondary school diplomas in teacher training awarded under the pre-1974 system. Document 2.3 was issued in 1967 by the Pedagogical Institute, which the document states to be an Annex to the National Pedagogical University. Immediately below this information, the document states that the student has completed all of the curriculum required in order to be awarded the *título de Maestra* (diploma or title of teacher, which in this case is a woman since the word ends in an "a"). The signatures on the document include those of a delegate from the Ministry of National Education, and various officials of the university and the institute. Document 2.4 is also a secondary school teacher training diploma. It was issued by the National Normal School for Young Men of Pasto and states that the student who was awarded the diploma successfully passed all the education officially required for teacher training students and has been awarded the *título de Maestro Superior* (title of teacher, in this case a man since *Maestro* ends in "o"). The document is signed by the *Rector* and Secretary of the school and by the Governor of the state and the Secretary of Education.

Document 2.5 represents a *título de Experto en Mecánica* (title of expert in mechanics) issued under the old system by the Don Bosco Center, operating under Resolution 3235 of September 20, 1963, of the Ministry of National Education. It states that the student, having satisfactorily completed secondary industrial education and passed the required exams in accord with Decree

No. 2.1. *Bachiller Académico* (Academic Secondary Diploma or Title) from a
Public Secondary School.

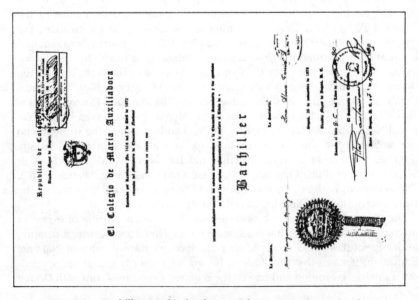

No. 2.2. *Bachiller Académico* from a Private Secondary School.

No. 2.3. *Maestra* (Secondary School Diploma in Teacher Training).

No. 2.4. *Maestro Superior* (Secondary School Diploma in Teacher Training).

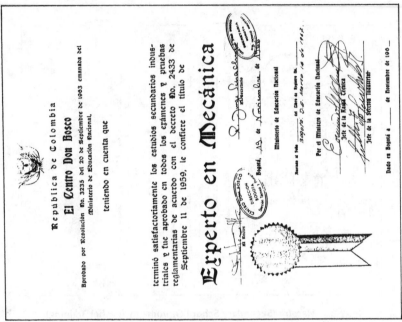

No. 2.5. *Experto en Mecánica* **(Expert in Mechanics).**

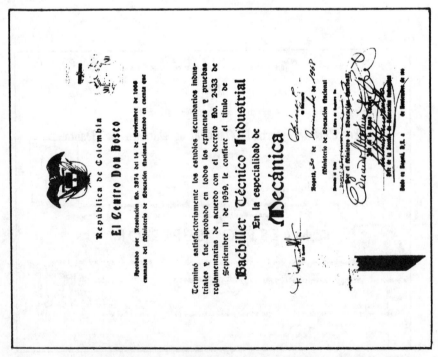

No. 2.6. *Bachiller Técnico Industrial* **(Technical Industrial Diploma), Specialization in Mechanics.**

2433 of September 11, 1959, has been granted this title. It is signed by the *Rector* and Secretary of the school, and by the Chiefs of the Technical and Industrial Sections of the Ministry. This title was granted upon completion of the basic cycle of education and represents nine years of education.

Document 2.6 is a *Bachiller Técnico Industrial* (technical industrial *Bachiller*) of the old system, also issued by the Don Bosco Center, but operating under Resolution 3874 of November 14, 1968. It states that the student has successfully completed secondary industrial education, with a specialization in mechanics. It also states that the student has passed the required exams under Decree 2433 of September 11, 1959, to earn this secondary diploma. Like Document 2.5, it is signed by various officials of the Ministry of National Education and of the school, and was awarded in Bogotá on November 30, 1968.

Document 2.7 is a sample *Bachiller* from an *Instituto Nacional de Enseñanza Media Diversificada*/INEM (comprehensive high school) named "Jorge Isaacs," in Cali. Note the place left for the specialization (*modalidad*) to be written in. This document dates from 1969, the year these experimental schools were opened; such documents are still being awarded under the current system. The document has places for the signatures of the Secretary of Education and school officials. It also has a place for the date of issue, place of registration, page number of the registration book, the number of the diploma, and the date and year of issue.

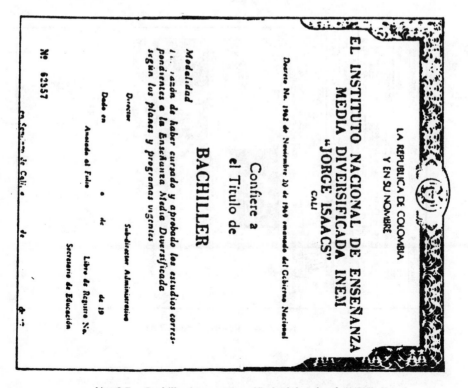

No. 2.7. *Bachiller* from a Diversified High School (INEM).

No. 2.8a.   **Secondary School Transcript.**

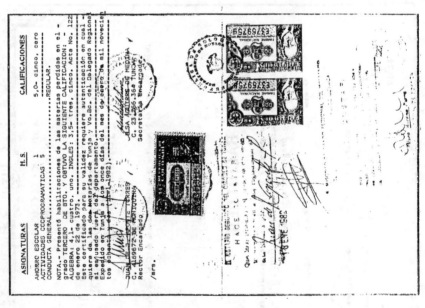

No. 2.8b.   **Reverse side of 2.8a.**

Document 2.8a and b is the front and reverse side of a secondary school transcript. Admissions officers should note carefully that this transcript from the Colegio de Boyacá in Tunja was issued during the period when the pre-1974 and the post-1974 grading systems overlapped (1972-73-74). It shows subjects (*asignaturas*), class hours (H.S. or *horas semana*) per week, and grades (*calificaciones*) received for the third, fourth, and fifth years of secondary school. The third (*tercero*) year and fourth (*cuarto*) year grades are on the old system, while those of the fifth (*quinto*) year are on the new system. It should also be noted that in the third year the student failed algebra (1.40) and English (2.63). The reverse side of the document shows that the student took make-up exams in algebra and English following these failures and then passed algebra with a 4.1 and English with a 3.5. The remaining information indicates that the document was registered as Document———of January 22, 1973. It was signed by the *Rector* and Secretary of the school, and was notarized.

Document 2.9 is a transcript of the sixth, or final, year of secondary school. It was issued in 1982. Note the various methods of writing grades by comparing Documents 2.8 and 2.9.

Documents 2.10 and 2.11 are included in the section on Non-Formal/Vocational Education in this chapter.

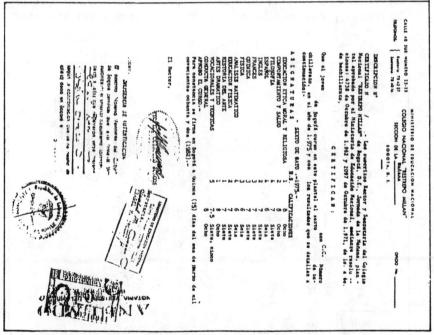

No. 2.9. Transcript of the Sixth, or Final, Year of Secondary School.

Non-Formal/Vocational Education

SENA

The Servicio Nacional de Aprendizaje/SENA (National Apprenticeship Service) has been operating in Colombia since 1957. A non-academic vocational training program, SENA is directed toward youths between the ages of 14 and 20. Neither secondary nor postsecondary education, this innovative program provides training to help workers perform more effectively on the job. To enroll, the student must be employed and have an equivalent of five years' elementary education, even though the program is non-academic.

The types of programs to be offered is determined through studies of the business community and its need for trained workers. A SENA program rarely is more than three years in length and is usually alternated equally with on-the-job training. SENA's facilities, equipment, and teachers are considered to be excellent.

As previously stated, the programs offered by SENA are in general non-academic and are vocationally oriented. For example, see Document 2.10, an Apprenticeship Certificate issued by SENA. This document states that the National Apprenticeship Service/SENA certifies that the apprentice is able to perform the trade of *operador máquinas herramientos* (machine tool operator). The courses passed include manual adjustment, mechanical adjustment,

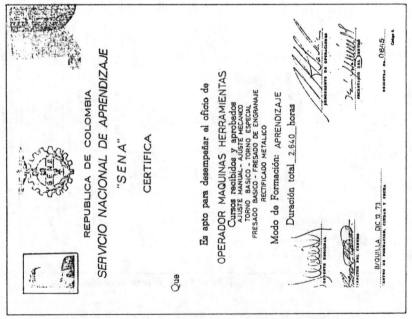

No. 2.10.   Apprenticeship Certificate Issued by SENA.

basic lathe, special lathe, basic milling, gear milling, and metal rectifying. The *modo de formación* (mode of training) is *aprendizaje* (apprenticeship), the hours spent in training 2640. The document is signed by the regional manager, the assistant manager of operations, and the Director and the Secretary of the center. There is a register number and a code.

The most important certificate offered by SENA is the *Certificado de Aptitud Profesional*/CAP (certificate of professional aptitude). To qualify for the CAP, apprentices must have completed basic secondary education (9 years). Document 2.11 is an example of a CAP issued to a *Barman-Mesero* (bartender-waiter). The *áreas aprobadas* (approved areas of study) include the following: *tecnología práctica de comedores y cocina* (practical technology of the dining room and kitchen); *enología bebidas y licores* (the art of making drinks and liqueurs); *idiomas* (languages); *ventas* (sales); *cultura general* (general culture); and *ética y desarrollo humano* (ethics and human development).

The CAP, when followed by two years of employment supervised by SENA, leads to a certificate awarded by ICFES, the *Certificado de Equivalencia del Grado de Bachiller* (the certificate of equivalence of the *Bachiller* diploma). The certificate of equivalence gives entry to Levels 1 and 2 of higher education. The norms governing the awarding of the certificate of equivalence are defined by Decree 80 of 1980.

Decree 80 states categorically that the certificate of equivalence does not reach the caliber of the *Bachiller*. It also states that it is different from the *Bachiller* conferred upon students who have passed the *examen de validación del Bachillerato* (examination by validation showing completion of secondary

No. 2.11. *Certificado de Aptitud Profesional de—/* **CAP (Certificate of Professional Aptitude in—) (Bartending and Waiting on Tables), Issued by SENA.**

school), which is said by Decree 80 to be the equivalent of the ordinary *Bachiller*.

SENA is funded by a 2% payroll tax on industrial firms employing 10 or more workers and having capital equaling $2,500 U.S. It is linked with both the private sector and the government through its National Board of Directors. Aside from the payroll tax, SENA receives funding from the sale of goods manufactured at the institutions, from fines resulting from labor code violations, from contracts with public and private groups or businesses for implementing specialized programs benefitting them directly, and from a .5% levy on salaries and wages paid by government agencies for specific accelerated training programs.

The broad base of funding for SENA elicits guidance from many sectors of the community. Also, the SENA programs are constantly being evaluated and revised to meet the changing needs of the people and the economy.

With headquarters in Bogotá, and regional offices in each of the 23 states, SENA has plans for increasing its regional services. Other plans include the following: the development of training programs for the unemployed; assistance for businesses and industries in order that they might meet the standard required for their employees to participate in SENA programs; and added programs of study, including those pertaining to tourism, hotel management, food processing, mechanized agriculture, and middle and high level technical training.

Chapter Three

Higher Education

The System in General

For most of its history, Colombia's system of higher education has been dominated by traditional style universities modeled on those the Spanish settlers had known in Europe. The first Colombian university, Santo Tomás, was founded in the city of Bogotá in 1573 with the colonization of Nueva Granada, a large area which included what is now Colombia, Venezuela, Panamá, and Ecuador. Santo Tomás was followed by the Pontificia Universidad Javeriana in 1622, and the Colegio Mayor de Nuestra Señora del Rosario in 1653.

Until fairly recently, higher education was offered almost entirely by traditional universities, which served a small and select group of the population. Gradually over the last half century the number of universities has grown, and in the last 20 years has almost tripled. In 1983 there were 113 university-level institutions as opposed to 40 institutions legally approved to award degrees in 1973.[1]

The newer universities have in some cases emulated models other than the traditional universities, and more government control has been exercised over institutions of higher education, including universities, in recent years. Of even more importance has been the establishment of other types of institutions of higher education, most of which are directed toward technological and practical training. These changes have come about in response to the increasing and unrelenting demand for education by all sectors of Colombian society.

Reforms of higher education in Colombia are carried out by the Instituto Colombiano para el Fomento de la Educación Superior/ICFES (Colombian Institute for the Promotion of Higher Education). This agency, created by Decree 3638 of 1964, is charged with regulating and inspecting all matters related to higher education.

Decree No. 80 of 1980

The most important and far reaching of the reforms of recent years was the issuing of El Decreto Extraordinario No. 80 (hereafter called Decree 80) by the

---

1. Ralph M. Henderson, *Colombia: A Guide to the Academic Placement of Students from Colombia in Educational Institutions in the United States*, World Education Series (Washington, D.C.: American Association of Collegiate Registrars and Admissions Officers, 1974), pp. 8-9.

29

Ministry of National Education on July 22, 1980. The decree brought significant change to the higher education system and gave legality to certain standards already in existence.

The stated objectives of Decree 80, which reflect the continuing social and educational change in Colombia, are selectively summarized as follows: to use education to bring about a more just society able to participate in the international community with dignity; to make higher education accessible to all Colombians who meet the legal requirements; to bring those from the economically marginal urban and rural areas, as well as the indigenous population, into the system; to assist institutions and programs in meeting minimum academic, scientific, and administrative standards; to contribute to the development of preceding educational levels; to promote the scientific and pedagogical education of researchers and teachers; and to facilitate the transference of students from one type of educational program or institution to another.

The Most Significant Reforms of Decree 80

Decree 80 both changed and defined many aspects of the system of higher education. The reform which may have the greatest impact is that which officially established four levels of higher education. The four levels, which will be discussed in separate sections in this chapter, are the following:
1. *Formación Intermedia Profesional*/FIP (intermediate professional studies);
2. *Formación Tecnológica*/FT (technological studies);
3. *Formación Universitaria*/FU (university level studies);
4. *Formación Avanzada o de Postgrado* (graduate studies).

Another reform of Decree 80 that may have important consequences if fully implemented is a new official unit of measure for coursework completed. It is called *Unidad de Labor Académico*/ULA (unit of academic work). ULAs will be discussed later in this chapter under "Credit Systems."

Other important aspects of Decree 80 deal with admission to institutions of higher education. The various articles pertaining to admission are discussed below under "Admission."

Undergraduate Education

Admission

All students who wish to enter an institution of higher education must hold a *Bachiller* (secondary school diploma). They must also pass *El Examen de Estado* (The State Examination), which is discussed below under a separate heading.

Resolution 2746 of Decree 80 deals with admission to higher education. Article 1 states that a *Bachiller* in any of the *modalidades* (specializations) established by Decree 1419 of 1978 is required for entry to any of the three undergraduate levels of higher education. It also states that the *Normalista*

Superior and *Maestro Superior* (teacher training diplomas on the secondary level or titles) are equivalent to the *Bachiller* for admission purposes.

After stating that all higher education institutions require the *Bachiller* for entry, Article 2 then singles out two secondary level diplomas for special mention. These are the *Certificado de Equivalencia del Grado de Bachiller* (certificate of equivalence of the *Bachiller* diploma) and the *Bachiller* conferred upon those who pass the *examen de validación del Bachillerato* (validation examination showing completion of secondary school) of the Servicio Nacional de Pruebas (National Testing Service) of ICFES. Article 2 says that the certificate of equivalence is sufficient only for entry to the first and second levels of higher education, *Formación Intermedia Profesional* (intermediate professional studies) and *Formación Tecnológica* (technological studies). It then states that the certificate of equivalence not only is not equal to a *Bachiller* but that it is "different" from the *Bachiller* obtained upon passing the examination by validation. In summary, there are two types of *Bachiller*, that awarded upon the successful completion of secondary school and that awarded upon passing the *examen de validación*. Both types of *Bachiller* give equal access to all levels of higher education. The certificate of equivalence, on the other hand, is precisely what its name suggests, a title which for legal purposes in Colombia is the equivalent of completion of secondary school.

Both the certificate of equivalence and the examination by validation are discussed in Chapter 2, the former under "Non-Formal/Vocational Education," and the latter under "Documents—Current and Pre-1974."

Admission Prior to 1980. Before Decree 80, as now, it was necessary to have a *Bachiller* in order to apply for entry to most institutions of higher education. But at that time the requirement was policy set by the individual universities, not national law. Decree 80 legalized this long-term practice.

The student also had to pass an entrance examination, but the type of examination depended upon the individual university. Some universities administered The State Examination (discussed in the next section) of the Servicio Nacional de Pruebas (National Testing Service) of ICFES, while others gave their own examination. Some institutions required both. It may be that some non-university institutions of higher education required neither, but this would have been uncommon.

El Examen de Estado (The State Examination)

Under Decree 2343 of 1980, *El Examen de Estado* (The State Examination) is required for entry to any level or type of higher education institution in Colombia. The State Examination is prepared by ICFES and administered through the Servicio Nacional de Pruebas (National Testing Service). Each institution must require a minimum grade on the examination and weight the results in accordance with the academic requirements of the corresponding program. In other words, the results of these exams are independently interpreted by each institution which then makes its selection based on quotas.

In addition to the official requirements set by Decree 80, institutions of higher education may have other entry requirements of their own. These might include, besides examinations, consideration of the student's secondary record, and an interview. However, institutions of higher education are required to explain their system of admission to ICFES, indicating the respective weight assigned to The State Examination and the other examinations they require, and their relative importance.

Anyone applying to an institution of higher education must verify before registering that The State Examination was passed at the minimum grade required by the respective university.

The State Examination is an objective test of aptitude and general knowledge. See Table 3.1 for subjects, number of questions, and time allowed for each question on the exam.

Table 3.1. **List of Subjects and Time Required for Each on *El Examen de Estado* (The State Examination)**

Session	Area	Test	Number of Questions	Time Hrs.	Mins.
First	Sciences	Biology	65	1	—
		Chemistry	50	1	—
		Physics	50	1	—
		Total Session	165	3	
Second	Language	Verbal Aptitude	82	1	15
		Spanish & Literature	60	1	—
	Elective*			—	45
		Total Session†		3	
Third	Mathematics	Math Aptitude	37	1	—
		Mathematical Theory including Geometry	37	1	—
	Social Sciences	Geography	40	—	—
		History	46	1	15
		Behavior & Health	34	—	—
		Total Session	194	3	15

SOURCE: ICFES—Servicio Nacional de Pruebas (Bogotá, February 1983).

*Electives may vary according to field of study.

†Total depends upon field of study.

Measurement of Credit/Transfer Credit Practices

Before Decree 80, all Colombian institutions of higher education measured coursework completion in credit hours and number of years of study. Since Decree 80, all institutions are required to measure coursework in *Unidades de Labor Académica*/ULAs (units of academic work). An ULA is defined as 1 hour of class time plus 2 hours of practical application plus 3 hours of independent academic work, either theoretical or practical, under direct supervision. ULAs have been used to establish minimum curriculum standards for the four levels of higher education as follows:

Title or Degree	Minimum Number of ULAs Required
Técnico Profesional Intermedio (intermediate professional technician)	1400, broken down as follows: 20-30% in science; 60-70% in supervised practice; at least 10% in the humanities.
Tecnólogo (technologist)	2100, broken down as follows: 30-40% in science; 50-60% in supervised practice; at least 15% in the humanities.
Tecnólogo Especializado (specialized technologist; program expected to begin functioning in 1984.)	900, in addition to the 2100 required for the *Tecnólogo*.
Licenciado or comparable first university degree such as a *título de* (title of), *Ingeniero* (engineer), or *Economista* (economist), etc.	3200. The kind of ULAs required for programs leading to the *Licenciado* or a comparable degree depends upon the individual program and university. The thesis may account for as little as 2.5% or as much as 10% of the required 3200 ULAs.[2]
Especialista (specialist; post-*Licenciado* or other first degree)	600, of which 50% must be in practical areas.
Magister (master's degree)	800, of which 30% must be in research.
Doctor	1600, which may include ULAs previously earned in a master's program; 40% must be earned through independent research and work.

From looking at curriculums from all types of institutions of higher education, as well as at transcripts, it would appear that the Colombian schools have been slow to adopt the ULA system. Only one curriculum in this volume shows ULAs as a measurement of credit (see Table 3.4). Because so little information on ULAs was available from individual institutions, credit hours have been used where necessary in this volume. Nevertheless, under Decree 80, the use of ULAs continues to be required.

Transfer Credit Practices. The acceptance of transfer credit by Colombian institutions of higher education depends upon several things: the program into which the student wishes to transfer, its number of openings, and the student's qualifications for that program. The student's credits will be evaluated on a course-by-course basis with the amount of credit allowed dependent upon the individual university and program.

Students from Level 1 of higher education, *Formación Intermedia Profesional/* FIP (intermediate professional studies), are eligible only for transfer into

---

2. Decree 80.

programs of Level 2, *Formación Tecnológica*/FT (technological studies). Also, it is possible that FIP students accepted as transfer students into FT programs in selective institutions will be granted reduced transfer credit.

Students who complete part or all of an FT program offered at a university might possibly transfer into a technological program within the same university or some other university and work toward a first university degree.

If the *Tecnólogo Especializado* (technological specialist) program is approved by ICFES (see later section of this chapter), FT graduates apparently will be accepted into the new program almost automatically. The title of *Tecnólogo Especializado* is planned to be equivalent to a five-year first degree.

Students do not appear to transfer casually from one university to another in Colombia, nor is credit granted automatically. Perhaps the fact that Decree 80 lists as one of its objectives the facilitation of student transfer from one type of educational program or institution to another is indicative that any kind of transfer is fairly uncommon.

Grading/Examinations

Grading. Practically all grading systems in Colombian higher education are based on a scale of 0.00 to 5.00 with 3.00 the lowest passing grade. Grades are recorded as whole numbers and decimal subdivisions, and the highest and lowest grades are practically never used.

Every student receives a numerical grade for each subject each semester. These grades are the result of a weighted average of several tests, homework, papers, and a final examination.

Even though the grading system in undergraduate programs of all institutions of higher education are uniform by law, the grade average varies somewhat with the *facultad* (college or school) in most universities.[3] These differences may be attributed to differences in traditions of the *facultad* rather than to the grading system. No statistical analysis has been done to determine just how wide the variations might be. See Table 3.2 for suggested grade equivalencies between the Colombian and U.S. systems of higher education.

Table 3.2. **Comparison of Grading Systems Used by Institutions of Higher Education in Colombia and the United States**

Colombian System	U.S. Equivalent
4.60-5.00 extremely high, very rarely attained	A+
4.00-4.59 excellent	A
3.50-3.99 good	B
3.00-3.49 sufficient, average	C
0.00-2.99 failure	F

3. The Spanish term *facultad* for faculty in this sense will be used throughout this volume.

Examinations. Examinations are held at the end of every semester in every subject. A student who makes a grade below 3.00 must take a re-examination (*examen de habilitación*). Most Colombian schools do not include the first failing grade in their determination of a student's average. On some transcripts the failure may be listed without special identification in a later term or year with the grade obtained on the re-examination. Some universities (e.g., Universidad de los Andes, Universidad Nacional de Colombia) enter on the transcript the yearly grade average (*promedio*) and the overall grade average (*promedio general de calificaciones*) upon completion of the total degree program.

Rankings among students are not made public, with the exception of those in the highest places at some schools. These students may be given a *Matrícula de Honor* (honor scholarship) or *Exención de Matrícula* (tuition waiver) for the next semester.

Undergraduate Degrees and Diplomas

The degrees and titles awarded in each of the levels of higher education under Decree 80 are discussed below.

Level 1 Awards. *Formación Intermedia Profesional*/FIP (intermediate professional studies) offers the *título de Técnico Profesional Intermedio en* _____/TPI (intermediate professional technician in _____). Level 1 studies are discussed in a separate section under "*Formación Intermedia Profesional* (Intermediate Professional Studies)/Level 1."

Document 3.1 shows a sample diploma that would be awarded to a student who had earned the title of *Técnico Profesional Intermedio en Ingeniería Industrial* (industrial engineering). The diploma is from the Centro Colombiano de

No. 3.1. *Técnico Profesional Intermedio en Ingeniería Industrial* (Intermediate Professional Technician in Industrial Engineering).

República de Colombia
Ministerio de Educación Nacional

Departamento del Valle del Cauca

Centro Colombiano de Estudios Profesionales
Resolución No. 2023 de Diciembre 18 de 1.982 por el Icfes.

Confiere el Título de:
Técnico Profesional Intermedio en

Administración y Finanzas
a

El Rector   El Decano   La Secretaria Académica

Cali,_____ de _____ de 19____

Gobernación del Departamento del Valle del Cauca
Anotado al Folio_____ del Libro de Registro No.____

Secretario de Educación

Santiago de Cali,

No. 3.2. *Técnico Profesional Intermedio en Administración y Finanzas* (Intermediate Professional Technician in Administration and Finance).

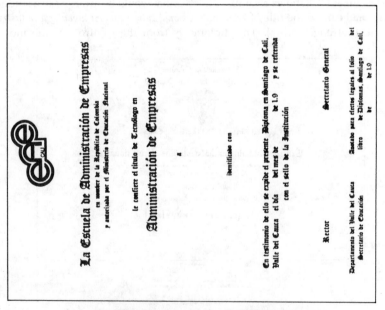

No. 3.3. *Tecnólogo en Administración de Empresas*
(Technologist in Business Administration).

Estudios Profesionales (Colombian Center of Professional Studies) in the Departamento (state) del Valle del Cauca. The program was *aprobado* (approved) by Resolution 1538 of February 14, 1979, by the Ministry of National Education. At the bottom of the page are places for the signatures of the *Rector*, the Dean, and the Secretary of the school, as well as for the Secretary of Education of the state.

Document 3.2 is the same kind of document from the same school. However, the program is approved under a different resolution, 2023 of December 16, 1982, by ICFES. This title is in *Administración y Finanzas* (administration and finance).

Level 2 Awards. *Formación Tecnológica*/FT (technological studies) offers the *título de Tecnólogo en* _____ (technologist in _____). The only FT title in Appendix A that deviates from this terminology is that of the *Regente en Farmacia* (registered pharmacist) at the Universidad de Antioquia. Level 2 studies are discussed in a separate section under "*Formación Tecnológica.*"

Document 3.3 is a sample Level 2 diploma from La Escuela de Administración de Empresas (The School of Business Administration), in Cali. Like all official higher education documents, it is authorized in the name of the Republic of Colombia and by authority of the Ministry of National Education. It states that the *título de Tecnólogo en Administración de Empresas* (technologist in business administration) is conferred, and a space is left for the name of the student. Below the place for the student's name, it is stated that the signatures of the officials and the stamp (*sello*) of the institution are proof of the date and place of issue, which is Santiago de Cali, Departamento del Valle del Cauca. There are places for the signatures of the *Rector* and General Secretary of the school, and for the Secretary of Education of the state. In the right-hand corner below is a place for the date the diploma is to be added, for legal purposes, to the "Book of Diplomas" of Cali, with a place for the page and the date.

Level 3 Degrees. The degrees of *Formación Universitaria* (university level studies) are somewhat more complicated than those of Levels 1 and 2. The first university degrees in Colombia are the *Licenciado* and comparable degrees that reflect the field in which they were received, such as *Físico* (physicist), *Ingeniero* (engineer), or *Médico*. Most of these first degrees that name the field are titles and would be preceded by the term *título de* (title of _____). (See Document 3.4.) However, some first university degrees are preceded by other terms such as *diplomado en* (diploma holder in _____), or *Maestro en* (master of some form of the arts). In some cases, only the name of the title received is given (see Document 3.5).

The *Licenciado* may be of two types: It may be a degree in education with a specialization in teaching a specific subject, usually at the secondary level, or it may be a degree in a non-teaching profession. Documents 3.6 and 3.7 are examples of a *Licenciado* in education (educational sciences in this case), the former with a specialization in biology and chemistry, the latter in the social sciences. Both are teaching degrees. A person who holds a *Licenciado* in biology and chemistry would be a "specialist" or "professional" in that field.

It should be noted that while the *Licenciado* and comparable first degrees are considered equivalent programs of study, the number of semesters of study required for each degree may vary from institution to institution. For example, the *título de Químico* may be 8 semesters in length at some universities and 10 in others.

Also, it should be remembered that some terms, particularly *título de _____*, are used at various levels of education (see Chapter Two).

Prior to 1980, the first degree usually was four years in length, although there were some three-year degrees (discussed under "Three-Year Degrees" in this section) and some that required more than four years. Since 1980, university-level institutions award a number of degrees of four to five, and in a few cases six, years' length. However, the most common university degree is the four-year *Licenciado*. It is the standard against which all other degrees of four or more years' duration are measured.

There are some first degrees that are peculiar to an individual university. For example, the Universidad Nacional de Colombia/UNC (National University of Colombia) offers a 12-semester program in medicine that leads to a *Doctor en Medicina*.

That institution also has a 10-semester program in veterinary medicine that leads to a *Doctor en Medicina y Veterinaria*, and a 9-semester program in dentistry that leads to a *Doctor en Odontología*. For specific degrees awarded by each institution of higher education, consult Appendix A.

Degrees considered comparable to the four-year *Licenciado* for legal purposes and for admission to graduate school include the following:

Abogado (lawyer)

Administrador de Comercio Exterior (foreign trade specialist)

Administrador de Empresas (business administrator)

Administrador de Hotelería y Turismo (hotel and tourism manager)

Administrador Marítimo (maritime administrator)

Administrador Público (public administrator)

Agrólogo/Agrícola (agricultural specialist)

Agrónomo (agronomist)

Antropólogo (anthropologist)

Arquitecto (architect)

Bacteriólogo (bacteriologist)

Bacteriólogo y Laboratorista Clínica (clinical bacteriologist)

Bibliotecólogo (librarian)

Biólogo (biologist)

Biólogo Marino (marine biologist)

Comunicador Social (public relations specialist)

Contador Público (public accountant)

Diplomado en Bellas Artes (diploma holder, fine arts)

Diplomado en Ciencias Políticas (diploma holder, political science)

Diplomado en Comercio Internacional (diploma holder, foreign trade)

Diplomado en Estudios Diplomáticos e Internacionales (diploma holder, diplomacy and international studies)

Diplomado en Filosofía y Letras (diploma holder, philosophy and letters)

Diplomado en Inglés
(diploma holder, English)

Diplomado en Letras
(diploma holder, letters)

Diplomado en Teología (theologian)

Director de Banda (band director)

Director de Coros (choral director)

Director de Orquesta
(orchestra conductor)

Diseñador Gráfico
(graphic designer)

Diseñador Industrial
(industrial designer)

Doctor en Medicina (physician)

Dr. en Medicina y Veterinaria
(veterinarian)

Dr. en Odontología (dentist)

Economista (economist)

Enfermera (nurse)

Estadística (statistician)

Farmacéutico (pharmacist)

Filósofo (philosopher)

Filósofo o Diplomado en Filosofía y Letras
(philosopher and diploma holder,
philosophy and letters)

Físico (physicist)

Fisioterapeuta
(physical therapist)

Fonoaudiólogo
(phonoaudiologist)

Geólogo (geologist)

Geotecnólogo (geotechnologist)

Gerente Hotelero y de Turismo
(hotel & tourism manager)

Historiador (historian)

Ingeniero (engineer)

Maestro en Artes Plásticas
(master of plastic arts)

Maestro en Bellas Artes
(master of fine arts)

Maestro en Cerámica
(master of ceramics)

Maestro en Composición Musical
(master of musical composition)

Maestro en Educación Musical
(master of musical education)

Maestro en Música (master of music)

Maestro en Pintura (master of painting)

Matemático (mathematician)

Médico (physician)

Médico Cirujano (surgeon)

Médico Veterinario (veterinarian)

Médico Veterinario y Zootecnista
(veterinarian and animal science
specialist)

Microbiólogo (microbiologist)

Oceanógrafo Físico
(physical oceanographer)

Odontólogo (dentist)

Optometra (optometrist)

Profesional en Ciencias Administrativas
(specialist in administrative sciences)

Profesional en Estudios Religiosas
(specialist in religious studies)

Profesional en Educación Familiar y Social
(professional in social and family
education)

Profesional en Filosofía y Letras
(specialist in philosophy and letters)

Profesional en Lenguas Modernas
(specialist in modern languages)

Profesor (professor)

Psicólogo (psychologist)

Químico (chemist)

Químico y Farmacéutico
(chemist and pharmacist)

Servidor Social (social worker)

Sociólogo (sociologist)

Teólogo (theologian)

(continued)

Terapeuta Ocupacional (occupational therapist)	*Veterinario y Zootecnista* (veterinarian and animal science specialist)
Trabajador Social (social worker)	*Zootecnista* (animal science specialist)

SAMPLE DOCUMENTS, LEVEL 3

Document 3.4 is a sample diploma from the Universidad Nacional de Colombia/UNC (National University of Colombia) that confers upon the student the *título de Químico* (chemist). This title is a first university degree. Below the title is a place for the name of the student. It is then stated that the respective stamps and signatures below, which include those of the Dean and Secretary of the *Facultad* of Science, the *Rector* of National University, and various other school officials, as well as the Minister of National Education, are witness to the fact that the diploma was awarded on May 4, 1973. Note in the right-hand corner that the diploma was registered on a certain page of the "Book of Diplomas," August 31, 1978.

Document 3.5 is a first degree awarded by a private university, Universidad de los Andes (University of the Andes), in Bogotá. The document states that the student, having complied with the academic requirements of the university (*"ha cumplido con los requisitos académicos exigidos por la Universidad"*), has been presented the diploma of *Ingeniero Mecánico* (mechanical engineer) by the Governing Council and the *Rector* of the university, through the authority vested in them. The document is signed and stamped by the various officials of the school and by the Mayor of Bogotá. It is registered on p. 33, Book 1.

Document 3.6 is a *Licenciado*. It was awarded by La Universidad Pedagógica Nacional (The National Pedagogical University) and states that the student, having passed the required studies, has been awarded the *Licenciado en Ciencias de la Educación, Especializado en Biología y Química* (*Licenciado* in educational sciences with a specialization in biology and chemistry). This diploma was awarded in Bogotá, June 19, 1974, and is signed and stamped by the usual officials of the school, and by the Mayor of Bogotá. It has been registered on p. 9 of the "Book of Diplomas."

Document 3.7 is a *Licenciado* awarded in the same field (educational sciences) as Document 3.6 but by a different school and with a different specialization. This document was awarded by the Universidad Santiago de Cali (the University of Santiago of Cali), a private university, by the *Facultad* of Educational Sciences (with the program approved by Resolution 8983 of November 7, 1974). The student's specialization is *Ciencias Sociales* (social sciences). Under the place left for the student's name, it is stated that the signatures of the school's Dean, *Rector*, and General Secretary, and of the state's Governor and Secretary of Education are witness to the fact that the diploma was granted in Santiago de Cali, Valley of Cauca, June 9, 1978.

No. 3.4. *Título de Químico*, Universidad Nacional de Colombia.

UNIVERSIDAD DE LOS ANDES

BOGOTA

REPUBLICA DE COLOMBIA

El Consejo Directivo y el Rector de la Universidad de los Andes

con las debidas autorizaciones legales y teniendo en cuenta que

ha cumplido con los requisitos académicos exigidos por la Universidad, le otorga con
los derechos, obligaciones y prerrogativas correspondientes, el presente Diploma de

Ingeniero Mecánico

El Rector

El Decano de la Facultad

El Presidente del Consejo Directivo

El Secretario General

ALCALDIA MAYOR DE BOGOTA D.E.
Anotado al Folio No. del Libro No.
EL SECRETARIO DE EDUCACION

Bogotá D.E. a de de 1981

REGISTRADO
LIBRO / FOLIO 35

Bogotá, 26 de agosto de 1.978

No. 3.5. *Diploma de Ingeniero Mecánico*, Universidad de los Andes.

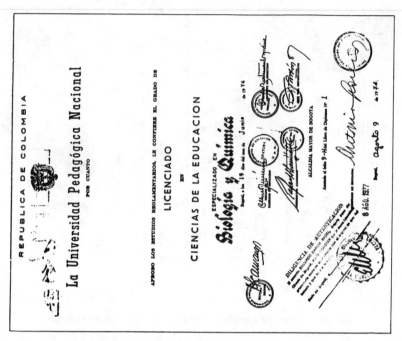

No. 3.6. *Licenciado en Ciencias de la Educación, Especializado en Biología y Química,* Universidad Pedagógica Nacional.

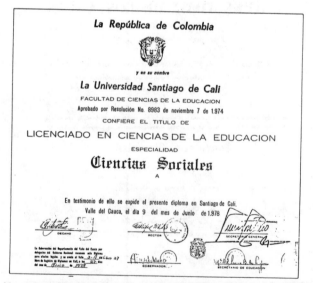

No. 3.7. *Licenciado en Ciencias de la Educación, Especialidad Ciencias Sociales,* La Universidad Santiago de Cali.

Three-Year Degrees

At the present time the only Colombian *Licenciatura* programs (those leading to the *Licenciado*) of less than eight semesters are three seven-semester programs offered by the Universidad Nacional de Colombia. The three programs lead to *Licenciados* in *Terapia del Lenguaje* (speech therapy); *Terapia Física* (physical therapy); and *Terapia Ocupacional* (occupational therapy).

Students who hold a three-year degree (old or new system) are not admissible to master's degree programs at Colombian universities under the present system. Under the old system they were admissible to the university where the first degree was granted in the same field of study in which the degree was earned.

Among the three-year university degrees offered in Colombia before 1980 were the following, listed with the universities that awarded them.[4]

Universidad Nacional de Colombia/UNC (National University of Colombia)	*Licenciado en Investigación Folklórica* (folklore investigation)
	Maestro de Capilla (chapel master)
	Estadístico (statistician)
Colegio Mayor de San Buenaventura (Higher College of San Buenaventura)[5]	*Licenciado en Filosofía* (philosophy)
Universidad Tecnológica de los Llanos Orientales (Technological University of the Eastern Llanos)[6]	*Licenciado en Enfermería* (nursing)

Diplomas—Pre-1980

The following diploma programs were offered before 1980 in Colombia, usually by non-university institutions of higher education or "other institutions of higher education," as they were classified by ICFES. Universities that offered any of the three programs leading to one of the titles are listed below under the individual descriptions of the programs.

- **Perito**—2-4 Semesters: These programs usually were offered in non-university institutions of higher education in such fields as accounting, secretarial work, design, etc. Most of the non-university higher educational institutions were private, and it was possible to enter at least one of these institutions (no longer in existence) after only 10 years of education. The entrance requirements for most of these schools were the *Bachiller* (secondary school diploma), the passing of an entrance exam, and an interview. A very few of these programs were offered in universities, one of which was the Universidad Pedagógica Nacional (National Pedagogical University), in

---

4. *Directorio de Universidades Colombianas*, ICFES, Bogotá, 1970-77.
5. This institution is not currently listed in the *Directorio*.
6. This three-year degree is now a *Tecnólogo en Enfermería*, a title granted at Level 2 of higher education.

Bogotá. This university offered a 4-semester program leading to the *Perito en Limitados Visuales* (working with those with visual handicaps). The program was offered during the day (*diurno*) and in the evening (*nocturno*).

- **Experto**—4-5 Semesters: These programs were offered in both non-university institutions of higher education and in universities, both public and private. To enter one of the programs, which covered a wide range of subjects, the student had to have a *Bachiller* and pass an entrance exam and an interview. In 1977, the universities offering the *Experto*, and the areas of study in which it was offered, were the following:

Fundación Universidad de Bogotá "Jorge Tadeo Lozano" (University Foundation "Jorge Tadeo Lozano" of Bogotá)—1) *Experto en Diseño Gráfico* (graphic design), daytime program, 5 semesters; 2) *Experto en Dibujo Arquitectónico y Decoración* (architectural design and decoration), daytime, 5 semesters.

Universidad Pedagógica Nacional (National Pedagogical University)—1) *Experto en Educación de Niños Excepcionales* (education of exceptional children), daytime and evening, 5 semesters; 2) *Experto en Educación Pre-Escolar* (preschool education), daytime and evening, 4 semesters; 3) *Experto en Pedagogía Musical* (teaching music), daytime and evening, 4 semesters.

Colegio Mayor de Cultura Femenina de Antioquia (Higher College of Feminine Culture of Antioquia)—*Experto en Orientación Familiar* (family orientation), daytime, 4 semesters.

Universidad Nacional de Colombia-Medellín (National University of Colombia-Medellín)—*Experto Forestal* (forestry expert), daytime, 4 semesters.

- **Técnico**—6 Semesters (one 7-semester evening program): These programs were offered both in non-university institutions of higher education and in universities. Among the universities offering this diploma in 1977, and the areas of study in which it was offered, were the following:

Pontificia Universidad Javeriana (Pontifical University of Javeriana), in Bogotá—1) *Técnico Superior en Dibujo Arquitectónico* (higher technician in architectural design), daytime, 6 semesters; 2) *Técnico Superior en Arte Publicitario* (public relations), daytime, 6 semesters.

Universidad del Valle, in Cali—1) *Técnico en Laboratorio Químico* (chemical laboratory technician), daytime, 6 semesters; 2) *Técnico en Laboratorio Médico* (medical laboratory technician), daytime, 6 semesters; 3) *Enfermera General* (general nurse), daytime, 6 semesters; 4) *Técnico en Administración de Empresas* (business administration), evening, 7 semesters; 5) *Topógrafo* (topographer).

Centro de Educación Superior del Norte del Valle, in Cartago—1) *Técnico Superior en Contabilidad* (accounting), daytime and evening, 6 semesters; 2) *Técnico en Administración Agropecuario* (agricultural administration), daytime, 6 semesters.

Colegio Mayor de Cultura Femenina de Antioquia, in Medellín—*Tecnólogo en Administración Turística* (tourist administration technician), daytime, 6 semesters.

Universidad Surcolombiana, in Florencia—1) *Técnico en Educación Pre-Escolar* (preschool education), evening, 6 semesters; 2) *Enfermero General* (general nurse), evening, 6 semesters.

Formación Intermedia Profesional (Intermediate Professional Studies)/Level 1

Programs in *Formación Intermedia Profesional*/FIP (intermediate professional studies), Level 1 of higher education studies, are usually four or five semesters in length. Many FIP programs are offered in the evening (*nocturno*), others during the day (*diurno*), and still others are offered at both times. Occasionally, an evening program will be spread out over a longer period of time than a daytime program, even though it will consist of the same number of class hours.

FIP programs are offered by public and private institutions. They cover a broad range of subjects including agriculture, art & design, business administration, telecommunications & electronics, etc.

The names of these schools also vary widely, although eight of the nine public FIP institutions have *instituto* (institute) as part of their names. Among the 65 private FIP institutions are *academias* (academies), *asociaciones* (associations), *centros* (centers), *corporaciones* (corporations), *fundaciones* (foundations), *escuelas* (schools), *colegios* ("colleges," a term usually associated with secondary education), *institutos*, etc. In other words, there is no all-encompassing term for the institutions which offer *Formación Intermedia Profesional* programs. Also, even though FIP studies usually are offered in institutions devoted solely to this type of education, there are some exceptions; a few FIP programs are offered in institutions devoted to *Formación Tecnológica* (technological studies), Level 2 of higher education, and a few are offered in universities, Level 3. For these exceptions, see Appendix A, Sections II, III.

For a curriculum in business administration at a private institution offering *Formación Intermedia Profesional*, see Table 3.3. Although no credit hours were available with this curriculum, according to Decree 80 anyone completing the program must have earned 1400 ULAs (discussed earlier in this chapter).

Table 3.3. **Business Administration Curriculum, *Formación Intermedia Profesional* (Intermediate Professional Studies), Level 1**

First Semester	Second Semester	Third Semester
Accounting I	Accounting II	Administration III
Administration I	Administration II	Cost Accounting I
Economics	Commercial Law	Finance Mathematics
Labor Law	Mathematics II	Industrial Psychology
Mathematics I	Microeconomics	Statistics II
Methodology	Statistics I	Tax Law

Fourth Semester	Fifth Semester
Cost Accounting II	Budget
Financial Analysis	Marketing Research
Industrial Relations	Production
Marketing	Salaries Administration
Project	Electives

SOURCE: Centro Colombiano de Estudios Profesionales (Cali, 1983).

The title or diploma awarded upon successful completion of an FIP program is that of *Técnico Profesional Intermedio en* _____/FIP (intermediate professional technician in _____). This title will appear on all diplomas from FIP programs regardless of the type of institution at which the program was offered. For examples of documents from an FIP program, see Documents 3.1 and 3.2. The documents are from the same institution. One title is in industrial engineering, the other in administration and finance. On each document, the number and date of the Resolution of Approval conferred upon the individual program by the Ministry of National Education appears under the institution's name.

Graduates of a program of intermediate professional studies have two options: they may enter a program of *Formación Tecnológica*/FT (technological studies; discussed in the next section) in any institution offering such a program, including some universities, or they may go to work. Credit from the FIP program cannot be transferred to other university programs.

See Section I, Appendix A, for an alphabetical listing of all institutions offering FIP programs exclusively. As noted above, a few FIP programs will also be found among the institutions listed in Sections II and III.

Another point to be noted in Section I of Appendix A is the recent establishment of five or six public FIP institutions in remote rural areas. These institutions evidently are so new that they are not listed in the *Directorio* of 1981. It would appear from this action that the Colombian government is attempting to use Level 1 of higher education to achieve one of the stated objectives of Decree 80: to bring the population of the economically marginal urban and rural areas, as well as the indigenous population, into the system.

Formación Tecnológica (Technological Studies)/Level 2

Programs in *Formación Tecnológica*/FT (technological studies), offered in public and private institutions, are usually six semesters in length, sometimes seven; there is one five-semester and one four-semester program (see Appendix A). The programs lead to the title of *Tecnólogo en* _____ (technologist in _____).

Among the public and private institutions offering technological studies listed in Appendix A, none has the term *Formación Tecnológica* in its name. They are called *institutos* (institutes), *politécnicos* (polytechnics), *corporaciones* (corporations), *colegios* (colleges), etc. In addition, FT programs are offered in some universities. There is no problem in recognizing credentials from such institutions, however, because almost all display the terms *título de Tecnólogo en* _____ (technologist in _____). For an example, see Document 3.3 in the earlier section on "Undergraduate Degrees and Diplomas"; this is a diploma from a private institution on which it is stated that the title of technologist in business administration is conferred ("*le confiere el título de Tecnólogo en Administración de Empresas*").

Among the FT programs offered are those in architecture, business, computer science, economics, engineering, and nursing. For curriculums in business administration and nursing, see Tables 3.4 and 3.5, respectively. Note in Table 3.4 that a thesis is required for the business administration program; none is shown in the nursing program. Note also in Table 3.4 the use of ULAs as a means of measuring coursework completed. All students are required to spend one year in obligatory work after completing the program. This year of work is not recorded on a student's transcript.

After the year of obligatory work, graduates of an FT program may transfer to a university and work toward a first university degree in a technological field, or they may enter the job market. A program especially designed as further study for FT graduates is awaiting approval by ICFES. For a description of the proposed program, see the next section, *"Tecnólogo Especializado."*

See Section II of Appendix A for an alphabetical listing of institutions offering *Formación Tecnológica*/FT. Also, see Section III for university-level institutions that offer FT programs. In Section III such programs are clearly identified.

Table 3.4. **Business Administration Curriculum, *Formación Tecnológica* (Technological Studies), Level 2**

Subject	hpw	ULAs	Subject	hpw	ULAs
First Semester			Second Semester		
Communication			Commercial Law	4	76
Techniques	2	23	Ecology	2	36
Economics I	4	67	Economics II	3	62
Fundamental			General Accounting II	4	59
Mathematics	4	67	General Admin. II	4	63
General Accounting I	4	61	Industrial Psychology	3	60
General Administration I	4	65			
Research Methods	3	42	Fourth Semester		
			Cost Accounting II	4	55
Third Semester			Decision Statistics	4	64
Cost Accounting I	4	58	Personnel		
Descriptive Statistics	4	73	Administration	4	56
Labor Law	3	60	Production Admin.	4	55
Process & Techniques			Public Administration	4	58
of Production	4	58	Sixth Semester		
Sociology	2	50			
Tax Law	3	46	Administration Auditing	3	51
			Business Workshop	5	68
Fifth Semester			Credit & Collection	3	39
Admin. Accounting	4	55	Financial Analysis	4	63
Data Processing	3	44	Marketing Research	4	56
Financial Mathematics	3	45	Professional Ethics	1	18
Marketing	4	63		121	1902
Organizational			Thesis		198
Develop.	2	24	Total		2100
Salaries Administration	4	62			

SOURCE: Corporación Escuela de Administración de Empresas (EAE), Cali, 1983.

Table 3.5. **Nursing Curriculum, *Formación Tecnólogo* (Technological Studies)**

Subjects	Credits	Subjects	Credits
First Semester		Second Semester	
Chemistry	4	Anatomy I	4
Ecology	4	Anthropology	3
General Psychology	4	Biology/Biochem./Nutrition	8
Introduction to Nursing I	4	English	2
Oral & Written Expression	3	Literary Appreciation	2
Technical English	3	Nursing II (Basics)	6
	22	Philosophy	1
			26
Third Semester			
Anatomy II	3	Fourth Semester	
Microbiology/Parasitology	5	Art Appreciation	2
Nursing III (Med. & Surg.):		Developmental	
Theory	3	Psychology	4
Practice	7	Nursing IV (Med. & Surg.):	
Physiology	5	Theory	3
	23	Practice	8
		Philosophy	1
Fifth Semester		Pharmacology	4
Administration (Theory)	3	Professional Ethics	3
Integral Course (Bio-			25
statistics/Epidemiology/			
Research)	6	Sixth Semester	
Nursing V (Psychiatry/		Family Health	4
Mental Health)	9	Nursing VII (Maternal/	
Nursing VI (Mgmt.		Infant)	18
Operating Rm.)	5		22
	23		
		Total:	151
Seventh Semester			
Nursing VIII (Nursing			
Services/Administration)			
Theory	4		
Practice	6		
	10		

Source: Instituto de Ciencias de la Salud/CES (Medellín, Colombia, 1981).

Tecnólogo Especializado

A two-year program leading to a degree of *Tecnólogo Especializado* (technological specialist) was expected to begin operation in Colombia in 1984. This program, if approved, will follow the three-year program of *Formación Tecnológica* (technological studies), described above, and the title awarded will be comparable to a first university degree. (This degree should not be confused with the graduate-level *Especialista* degree discussed under "Graduate

Education" in the last section of this chapter.)

Three institutes are scheduled to offer the program, one in Cali, and two in Medellín. Among other options, students who complete the program will be eligible to study toward a master's degree.[7]

Formación Universitaria (University Studies)/Level 3

University education has been called *Formación Universitaria* since Decree 80 established it as the third level of higher education in 1980. Despite the change in nomenclature, the universities continue to hold a prestigious position among Colombia's institutions of higher education. As previously stated, some universities trace their beginnings to the colonization of the continent, and for centuries were the only form of higher education in Colombia. Because of this heritage, traditions, especially among the older institutions, are strong, and change comes slowly.

Nevertheless, because of public demand for education at all levels, change is taking place in all of higher education including the universities. Although the universities still retain and value autonomy as a hallowed tradition, under Decree 80 few important decisions are left entirely to their discretion. For example, curriculums devised by the universities are subject to ICFES approval. Also, no school or department may be established without first obtaining a license from ICFES. However, in their day-to-day operations, the universities still enjoy considerable autonomy.

The Traditional Colombian University

One of the important characteristics of the traditional Colombian university is the importance of the *facultad* (literally, "faculty"; actually, in U.S. terms a school or college within a university). Within the Colombian *facultad*, there can be *escuelas* (schools), which in turn may be divided into *departamentos* (departments). How the *facultad* is divided would appear to be a matter of form rather than substance. What should be noted is the prominent role of the *facultad* within the university. The *facultad*, while not an autonomous entity, does have a certain existence quite independent of the university. All courses are taken within one *facultad*, and its teaching staff and students often identify more closely with the *facultad* than with the university itself.

Another characteristic of the traditional universities is a program of studies directed toward specific professions such as engineering, law, and medicine. (See Table 3.6 for enrollment figures for the various *facultades* and schools at Universidad Nacional de Colombia.) Curriculums tend to be rigid and specialized with few liberal arts courses, or electives. University administrators are said to believe that there is little need for electives because of the large body of basic, specific knowledge all students must master. A thesis is an important part of all programs (see discussion below).

---

7. Visit with officials of the Corporación Escuela de Administración de Empresas/ EAE, Cali, 1983.

The Thesis. Although almost all university *facultades* require a thesis (*trabajo de grado* or *tesis de grado*) in all degree programs, a few practically-oriented programs may not. The thesis is regarded as the culmination of a student's university career, and must represent original research. It may be either theoretical or practical in nature.

Table 3.6. **Enrollment at Universidad Nacional de Colombia by *Facultad* and by School, 1982**

Facultades/Schools	Enrollment	*Facultades*/Schools	Enrollment
Agronomy*	637	Law*	673
Arts		Medicine	
Architecture	895	Medicine	1,689
Conservatory	69	Nutrition/Dietetics	196
Fine Arts	393	Occupational Therapy	85
Industrial Design	204	Physical Therapy	186
Total	1,561	Speech Therapy	135
Dentistry*	950	Total	2,291
Economic Sciences		Nursing*	615
Accounting	784	Sciences	
Business Administration	680	Biology	446
Economics	887	Chemistry	426
Total	2,351	Geology	419
		Mathematics	137
Engineering		Pharmacy	661
Agricultural	217	Physics	138
Chemical	854	Statistics	144
Civil	759	*Licenciaturas:*	
Electrical	837	Biology †	74
Mechanical	920	Chemistry †	46
Systems	513	Mathematics †	28
Total	4,100	Physics †	5
Humanities and Social Science		Total	2,524
Anthropology	269	Veterinary Medicine and	
Education	195	Animal Science	
Foreign Languages	478	Animal Science	301
Philosophy	228	Veterinary Medicine	802
Political Science	241	Total	1,103
Psychology	350	Grand Total	19,299
Social Work	457		
Sociology	276		
Total	2,494		

SOURCE: Universidad Nacional de Colombia, Departamento de Registro y Matrícula, mayo 13 de 1982.

Facultades in which there are no subdivisions; enrollment is *facultad* total.

†Programs leading to the teaching degree in the field.

In the third or fourth year of study, the student chooses a thesis topic and makes initial contact with a *director* (thesis advisor). The topic must be approved and reported to the dean of the student faculty at least six months before the thesis is defended. The final draft must be submitted for review at least one month prior to its defense.

A majority of students work at least six months on the thesis, and many devote more than a year to its completion. (The number of ULAs awarded for the thesis may be as low as 2% or as high as 10%, the maximum allowed toward the degree.) The average length of the thesis is generally at least 200 pages.

The thesis must be defended before a committee composed of three to five faculty members and the director of the thesis, presided over by the dean. After successfully defending the thesis, the student is granted a degree.

University Types and Structure

Although most universities or university-level institutions have the word *universidad* as part of their name, quite a few do not. There are university-level institutions called *escuelas* (schools), *unidades* (units), *colegios* (colleges), *corporaciones* (corporations), *fundaciones* (foundations), and *institutos* (institutes). See Appendix A, Section III, for a complete alphabetical listing of university-level institutions.

Colombian universities may be grouped into two overall classifications: public and private. The public institutions may be further divided into the following categories, based principally on source of funding: national (*nacional*); state or sectional (*departamental*); and municipal (*municipal*). Brief descriptions of three institutions, two public and one private, along with course curriculums and documents, will show them to be more alike than different.

A National University. An example of a national university is the Universidad Nacional de Colombia/UNC (National University of Colombia), in Bogotá. Established in 1826 as the Universidad de Bogotá, the name was changed by Law 66 in 1967. The main campus is located in Bogotá, but there are also campuses in Medellín, Manizales, and Palmira, the first with three schools, and the latter two with one school each.

A large university with a diverse student body, National University faces frequent student strikes. These strikes often last for months on end, almost totally disrupting the academic functions of the university. The Bogotá campus is the most frequent location of these strikes, but at times other of the campuses are also affected.

Organized on the traditional lines discussed above, each *facultad* contains at least one school. The administrative head is the *Rector*, assisted by various boards and councils.

Most programs at UNC operate on a 14- to 16-week semester, and lead to a *Licenciado* or comparable first university degree after 8 or 10 semesters of study. (See the section on "Undergraduate Degrees and Diplomas" earlier in this chapter.) A complete listing of UNC degree programs, degrees awarded,

Table 3.7.   **Chemistry Curriculum, School of Chemistry,** *Facultad* **of Sciences,**
Universidad Nacional de Colombia

T = Theory		P = Practice	
Subjects	hpw	Subjects	hpw
First Semester		**Second Semester**	
Biology	5-T	Experimental Physics I	2-P
Biology Lab	4-P	General Chemistry II	4-T
Differential Calculus	7-T	General Chemistry Lab II	6-P
General Chemistry I	4-T	General Microbiology	3-T
General Chemistry Lab I	6-P	Gen. Microbiology Lab	3-P
Physics I	5-T	Integral Calculus	7-T
Third Semester		Physics II	5-T
Basic Analyt. Chemistry	3-T	**Fourth Semester**	
Basic Analyt. Chemistry Lab	3-P	Fundamental Methods &	
Differential Equations	5-T	Measurement I	4-P
Experimental Physics II	2-P	Gaseous Liquid & Solid	
Fundamental Theory	4-P	Systems	4-P
Inorganic Chemistry I	4-T	Inorganic Chemistry Lab	4-P
Physics III	5-T	Numerical Calculus	4-T
Fifth Semester		Physics Lab III	2-P
		Structural Inorganic Chem.	4-T
Electrochemistry & Kinetics	4-T	Structural Organic Chem.	4-T
Fundamental Methods &		**Sixth Semester**	
Measurement II	4-P	Industrial Analysis	4-P
Instrumental & Analyt.		Instrumental & Analyt.	
Chemistry I	4-T	Chemistry II	4-T
Instrumental & Analyt.		Instrumental & Analyt.	
Chemistry Lab I	4-P	Chemistry Lab II	4-P
Organic Chemistry Lab	6-P	Organic Analysis Lab I	9-P
Organic Reaction &		Organic Reaction &	
Mechanism I	4-T	Mechanism II	4-T
Seventh Semester		**Eighth Semester**	
Analysis Elements & Project		Agricultural Chemistry	4-T
in Applied Chemistry	6-P	Agricultural Chemistry Lab	4-P
Chemistry Technology I	4-T	Applied Physico-Chemistry	
Chemistry Technology Lab I	4-P	Lab	4-P
Descriptive & Dynamic		Biochemistry Lab	4-P
Biochemistry	4-T	Chemical Technology II	4-T
Industrial Organic Chemistry	4-T	Chemical Technology Lab II	4-P
Organic Analysis Lab II	6-P	Intro. to Quantum Chemistry	3-T
Ninth Semester		**Tenth Semester**	
Organic Synthesis Lab	8-P	Seminar	1-T
Elective I	4	Elective V	4
Elective II	4	Work on Thesis	—
Elective III	4		
Elective IV	4		
Work on Thesis	—		

SOURCE: Universidad Nacional de Colombia, El Consejo Superior Universitario, Acuerdo No. 215 de 1979 (22 de noviembre), Acta 45.

and the duration of study for each is shown in Appendix A.

See Table 3.7 for the curriculum in chemistry in the *Facultad* of Sciences at UNC. Note the work on the thesis in the ninth and tenth semesters. Note also that the first elective is offered in the ninth semester, and that the emphasis on the major subject is almost complete.

Document 3.4, a *título de Químico* (chemist), represents a first university degree in chemistry from UNC.

A State University. The Universidad del Valle in Cali is a state university established in 1945. The operation and organization of all state universities are governed by Decree 277 of 1958 which grants administrative autonomy and legality. Decree 277 established a system similar to that of the National University of Colombia, with differences only in form, not concept.

The function of all governing bodies of the state universities is patterned on those of UNC, with the *Rector* the highest executive authority.

Table 3.8 shows the economics curriculum in the School of Economics of the *Facultad* of Social and Economic Sciences, Universidad del Valle. Note that this is a four-year program. Note also the elective in the sixth and seventh semesters, and the two electives in the eighth semester. Although the work on the thesis does not show in the curriculum, it can be assumed that a thesis would have been required. The program leads to the *título de Economista* (economist).

Table 3.8. **Economics Curriculum, School of Economics, *Facultad* of Social and Economic Sciences, Universidad del Valle, 1981**

T = Theory			P = Practice		
Subjects	hpw		Subjects	hpw	
First Semester	T	P	Second Semester	T	P
English I	5	—	Calculus I	4	2
Fundamental			English II	5	—
Mathematics I	4	2	Intro. to Colombian		
History of Social			Economics II	4	—
Thought	3	—	Intro. to Social Science	3	—
Intro. to Colombian			Principles of Econ. II	3	2
Economics I	4	—			
Principles of			Fourth Semester		
Economics I	3	2	Linear Algebra I	4	—
			Macroeconomics I	3	2
Third Semester			Marxist Theory of		
Business Law	3	—	Economics II	4	—
Calculus II	4	2	Microeconomics II	3	2
Marxist Theory of			Statistics I	3	2
Economics I	4	—			
Microeconomics I	3	2	Sixth Semester		
Sociological Theory	3	—	Descriptive Economics	4	—
			Econometrics I	3	2
Fifth Semester			International Economics	4	—
Fiscal Economics &			Monetary Policy &		
Policy	4	1	Theory	4	—

(continued)

General Accounting	3	1	Elective	—	—
Microeconomics III	3	2	**Eighth Semester**		
Operational Research	3	1			
Statistics II	3	2	Colombian Economics	3	—
Seventh Semester			Economic Development II	4	—
Econometrics II	3	2	Economic Systems	4	—
Economic Development I	4	—	Elective	—	—
History of Colombian Economics	3	2	Elective	—	—
Project Evaluation	4	—			
Elective (1)	—	—			

SOURCE: Universidad del Valle, Consejo Directivo, Resolución 030, Marzo 18 de 1981.

A Private University. Pontificia Universidad Javeriana (Pontifical University of Javeriana), in Bogotá, is a Roman Catholic institution founded and directed by the Society of Jesus. Officially inaugurated as an academy in 1623, the school was closed in 1767 when the Jesuits were banished from the domain of Charles III. The university reopened in 1930. The largest Roman Catholic institution in Colombia, Javeriana has a total enrollment of 14,148, of which 1,138 are enrolled at a branch campus (*seccional*) in Cali. A summer course is offered from mid-June to mid-July.

As in the national and state schools, the highest ruling authority on the campus is the *Rector*, who is assisted by various councils. The school has 16 *facultades*, which offer 34 programs. The *facultades* are organized into divisions called *departamentos* (departments.)

Most of the university's funding comes from registration fees paid by students. A small portion is derived from the university's own revenue, and less than 1% comes from outside sources.

Tables 3.9, 3.10, and 3.11 show curriculums at Javeriana in business administration, electronic engineering, and nursing, respectively.

The five-year program in business adminstration leads to the title *Administrador de Empresas* (business administrator). Note the electives beginning in the sixth semester and continuing through the ninth. Note also that the tenth semester is devoted to practical training and the thesis.

The curriculum in electronic engineering, also five years in length, leads to the title *Ingeniero Electrónico* (electronics engineer).

The curriculum in nursing shown in Table 3.11 is four years in length. It leads to the title of *Enfermero(a)* (nurse). No thesis is shown on this program but it is possible that one was required.

Sample documents were not available from Javeriana, so Document 3.5 from another private university, the Universidad de los Andes, in Bogotá, has been substituted. This diploma in mechanical engineering is a first university degree.

Table 3.9. **Business Administration Curriculum, School of Business Administration,** *Facultad* **of Economic Sciences and Administration, Pontificia Universidad Javeriana, 1981-83**

Subjects	Credits	Subjects	Credits
First Semester		Second Semester	
General Economics	3	Administration Theories	3
Introduction to Business		Mathematics II	4
Administration	3	Microeconomics	3
Mathematics I	4	Political Science	2
Psychology	3	Religious Sciences I	2
Research Methodology I	3	Research Methodology II	2
Statistics I	3	Statistics II	3
Total	19	Total	19
Third Semester		Fourth Semester	
General Accounting I	3	General Accounting II	3
Management Theory &		Money & Banking	3
Practice	4	Operation Research	3
Mathematics III	3	Organization: Its Structure &	
Microeconomics	3	Function	4
Principles of Business Law	2	Religious Sciences II	2
Statistics III	3	Sociology	3
Total	18	Total	18
Fifth Semester		Sixth Semester	
Cost Accounting	3	Commercial Law I	2
International Commerce	3	Human Resources I	3
Labor Law	2	Marketing I	4
Legal Environment of		Research Project I	3
Business	3	Systems Analysis II	4
Operational Management I	4	Elective I	3
Systems Analysis I	4	Total	19
Total	19		
		Eighth Semester	
Seventh Semester		Finance II	3
Commercial Law II	2	Operational Management II	4
Finance I	3	Organizational Development	3
Human Resources II	3	Religious Sciences III	2
Management	3	Research Project II	3
Marketing II	4	Tax Law	2
Elective II	3	Elective III	3
Total	18	Total	20
Ninth Semester		Tenth Semester	
Colombian Economics:		Practical Training*	—
Operational Management III	4	Thesis*	—
Politics of Business	3		

(continued)

Relation Between Business &	
State	3
Religious Sciences IV	2
Thesis Research	2
Elective IV	3
Total	17

SOURCE: Pontificia Universidad Javeriana, *Catálogo General, 1981-83* (Bogotá, D.E., Colombia).
*Credits unspecified in university catalog.

Table 3.10. **Electronic Engineering Curriculum, *Facultad* of Engineering, Pontificia Universidad Javeriana, 1981-83**

Subjects	Credits	Subjects	Credits
First Semester		Second Semester	
Calculus I	4	Calculus II	4
Design	3	Introduction to a	
Introduction to Engineering	2	Programming Language	3
Physics I	4	Linear Algebra	3
Elective (Religious Sciences)	2	Material & Workshop	3
Total	15	Physics II	4
		Elective (Humanities)	2
Third Semester		Total	19
Calculus III	3		
Physics III	4	Fourth Semester	
Theory of Differential		Devices	4
Equations	3	Electric Circuit Analysis II	3
Electric Circuit Analysis I	3	Electromagnetic Theory	3
Elective (Humanities)	2	Electronics I	3
Elective (Religious Sciences)	2	Mathematical Methods in	
Total	17	Engineering	3
		Total	16
Fifth Semester			
Electric Circuit Analysis III	3	Sixth Semester	
Electronics II	3	Dynamics Systems Analysis	3
Electronics Lab I	3	Electronics III	3
Fields & Waves Theory	3	Electronics Lab II	3
Probability & Process	3	Electrotechnics	3
Special Methods of		Signal Theory Analysis	3
Computation	3	Elective (Religious Sciences)	2
Total	18	Total	17
Seventh Semester		Eighth Semester	
Communication Systems	3	Administration I	3
Electrical Pulses	3	Digital Computers	3
Electronics Lab III	3	Electronic Controls	3
Logical Circuits	3	Electronics Lab IV	3
Propagation of Waves	3	Industrial Electronics	3

Seminar		2	Technical Elective		3
	Total	17		Total	18

Ninth Semester			Tenth Semester		
Administration II		3	Professional Legislation		2
Professional Ethics		2	Thesis		6
Technical Electives		12	Technical Electives		6
	Total	17		Total	14
				Grand Total	168

SOURCE: Pontificia Universidad Javeriana, *Catálogo General, 1981-83* (Bogotá, D.E., Colombia).

Table 3.11.   **Nursing Curriculum, *Facultad* of Nursing, Pontificia Universidad Javeriana, 1981-83**

Subject	Credits	Subject	Credits
First Semester		Second Semester	
Science Courses: Biology,		Anatomy	3
Math, Organic Chemistry	14	Basis of Nursing Care	3
Introduction to Nursing		General Psychology	3
Profession	2	General Sociology	3
Philosophy	2	Methods of Teaching	3
Total	18	Religion I	2
		Research Methodology	2
Third Semester		Total	19
Developmental Psychology	4		
Introduction to Nursing Care		Fourth Semester	
in Health Sector	5	Microbiology	5
Physiology	4	Nursing Care in the Medical-	
Religion II	2	Surgical Sector I	6
Sociology & Culture	3	Physiopathology I	4
Total	18	Religion III	2
		Social Psychology	2
Fifth Semester		Total	19
Nursing Care in the Medical-			
Surgical Sector II	7	Sixth Semester	
Pharmacology	4	Maternal Child Nursing Care	12
Physiopathology II	3	Professional Ethics	2
Research Principles Applied		Research Dimension in	
to Epidemiology	3	Nursing	3
Total	17	Total	17
Seventh Semester		Eighth Semester	
Administration of Nursing		Design of Nursing Curriculum	3
Care Services & Teaching	15	Nursing Care in the Rural	
Nursing Care in Mental		Areas	8
Health & Psychiatry	6	Total	11
Total	21		
		Grand Total	140

SOURCE: Pontificia Universidad Javeriana, *Catálogo General, 1981-83* (Bogotá, D.E., Colombia).

Graduate Education

Under Decree 80, the fourth level of higher education is called *Formación Avanzada o de Postgrado* (graduate studies). Although the advancement of graduate education is not mentioned specifically among the stated objectives of Decree 80 (see "Decree No. 80 of 1980" earlier in this chapter), certain of the objectives would appear to require more and better graduate programs. For example, one objective is to "promote the scientific and pedagogical education of researchers and teachers," a task generally accomplished at the graduate level.

Historically, the term *postgrado* has had a broad and somewhat vague meaning in Colombia. Thus, any course of study taken after the first university degree (a *Licenciado* or a comparable first university degree) was considered a graduate program. This included diploma courses in various fields of study, among them teacher training, short courses or extension courses, seminars for executives, and, of course, programs leading to advanced degrees. Under Decree 80, ICFES seems to be trying to define the status of graduate education more clearly.

Three types of graduate programs are offered in Colombia: *Especialista* (specialist); *Magister, Magister Scientiae, Maestría,* or *Master* (various forms used for the master's degree); and the *Doctor* (doctoral). Despite the various types of programs offered, relatively few universities offer graduate programs, and only one, the Pontificia Universidad Javeriana in Bogotá, offers a *Doctor* degree. See Table 3.12 for all of the graduate programs offered at Javeriana. See Appendix A for graduate programs offered by the individual universities.

Table 3.12. **Graduate Programs, Pontificia Universidad Javeriana, 1983**

Especialista (Specialist) Programs			
Facultad of Dentistry	Credits	*Facultad* of Medicine	Years
Endodontics	35	Anesthesiology	2
Orthodontics	35	General Surgery	3
Periodontics	35	Gyneco-Obstetrics	3
Stomatology	35	Internal Medicine	3
		Neurology	3
Facultad of Law (Legal and Socio-Economic Sciences)		Opthalmology	3
		Orthopedics &	
Family Law	15	Traumatology	4
Labor Law	15	Otorhinolaryngology	3
		Pathology	3
		Pediatrics	3
		Psychiatry	3
		Radiology	3

Magister (Master's) Programs

Facultad of Interdisciplinary Studies	Credits	Facultad of Philosophy and Letters	Credits
Economics	30	History	30
Educational Research &		Literature	30
Technology	30	Philosophy	30
Health Administration	30		
Political Science	30	Facultad of Science	
Population & Demography	30	Biology	30
		Microbiology	30
Facultad of Law (Legal and Socio-Economic Sciences)		Nutrition	30
Commercial Securities	30	Facultad of Theology	
Insurance	30	Theology	30
Facultad of Philosophy			
Philosophy	30		

Doctor (Doctoral) Programs

Facultad of Canon Law*		Facultad of Philosophy and Letters	
Canonic Law	45	History	80
Facultad of Philosophy		Literature	80
Philosophy	80	Philosophy	80
		Facultad of Theology	
		Theology	70

SOURCE: Office of Inter-Institutional Relations, Pontificia Universidad Javeriana (Bogotá, February, 1983).

*To enter this facultad, it is usually necessary to be a priest or law school graduate.

Admission to Graduate Programs. The basic requirement for entry to *Especialista* (specialist) or *Magister* (master's) programs is either the *Licenciado* or a comparable first university degree, depending upon the program and field. An entrance examination is a common second requirement. Also, preference is usually shown to those applying to a program offered by the same university that awarded the student's first degree. Students who wish to do graduate study in a field different from that of the first degree may be required to take some prerequisite courses. The *Magister* is normally required for entry to a *Doctor* program, although occasionally a student will be admitted immediately following the first degree.

Grading. For a description of grading systems in institutions of higher education, see the section on undergraduate "Grading/Examinations" earlier in this chapter. Most institutions offering graduate programs use the same grading scale at the graduate level that they use at the undergraduate level, although there are a few exceptions. However, the minimum passing grade is much higher at the graduate level, 3.5 or higher.

Especialista (Specialist) Programs

Especialista (specialist) programs are usually offered in practical or applied disciplines such as medicine and dentistry. These programs are often one year in length, although there are exceptions, especially in the field of medicine, where programs may require up to four years for completion (up to one-half of such programs may be devoted to a period of residency in a hospital). Most of the specialist programs offered at Universidad Pontificia Javeriana are in medical fields. (See Table 3.12.)

Despite the fact that specialist programs frequently are associated with medical or health fields, they are offered in other fields of study including business administration, chemistry, education, engineering, and law. In keeping with their practical orientation, specialist programs usually do not require any research or a thesis. In some institutions or *facultades*, some courses may be applied toward either a specialist or a master's program. The title awarded in all specialist programs is that of *Especialista*.

The following *Especialista* programs in medicine include postgraduate clinical experience which in the United States would lead to board certification: *Anestesia y Reanimación; Anestesiología; Anestesiología, Reanimación y Cuidado Intensivo; Cardiología; Cirugía; Cirugía Cardiomuscular; Cirugía General; Cirugía Infantil; Cirugía Pediátrica; Cirugía Plástica; Cirugía Toráxica; Dermatología; Endoscopia Digestiva; Gastroenterología; Ginecología; Ginecología y Obstetricia; Gineco-Obstetricia; Gineco-Obstetricia y Patología; Hematología; Medicina Física y Rehabilitación; Medicina Interna; Nefrología; Neumología; Neurocirugía; Neurología; Neumología; Oftalmología; Ortopedia; Ortopedia y Traumatología; Otorrinolaringología; Patología; Patología Infecciosa; Pediatría; Psiquiatría; Radiodiagnóstico; Radiología; Radioterapia; Rehabilitación; Urología.*

In dentistry and nursing, *Especialista* programs that include postgraduate clinical experience are offered in the following areas: Dentistry—*Estomatología Pediátrica, Odontopediatría Clínica, Ortodoncia Preventiva (Estomatología Pediátrica),* and *Patología Oral (Estomatología).* Nursing—*Enfermería Cardiorespiratoria,* and *Enfermería en Salud Mental.*[8]

Magister (Master's) Programs

Programs leading to the *Magister, Magister Scientiae, Maestría,* or *Master* (all terms for the master's degree) require a minimum of two years for completion. The principal difference between the specialist programs and those leading to the master's is an emphasis on research in the latter. See Tables 3.13 and 3.14 for curriculums of master's programs at two universities. Table 3.13 shows the curriculum leading to the *Magister en Extensión para Desarrollo Rural*

---

8. Information supplied by Mary Jane Ewart, State Education Department, the University of the State of New York, Albany, New York.

Table 3.13. **Curriculum, *Magister en Extensión para Desarrollo Rural* (Master's of Rural Development Extension), Pontificia Universidad Javeriana**

Subjects	Semester Credits	Subjects	Semester Credits
First Semester		Second Semester	
Human Ecology	3	Rural Administration	3
Methods in Social Research	3	Rural Economics	3
Rural Sociology	3	Rural Education in Extension	3
Social Statistics	3	Social Communication	3
Total	12	Total	12
Third Semester		Fourth Semester	
Community Development	3	Master's Thesis	6
Electives*	2		
Seminar on Thesis	1		
Total	6	Grand Total	36

SOURCE: Pontificia Universidad Javeriana, *Facultad* of Interdisciplinary Studies (Bogotá, February, 1983).

*Electives: Ecological Development, Environmental Economics, Environmental Planning, Geography of Rivers, Group Dynamics, Mass Media, Social Anthropology.

Table 3.14. **Curriculum, *Magister en Administración Educacional* (Master's in Educational Administration), Universidad del Valle**

Subjects	Trimester Credits	Subjects	Trimester Credits
Administrative Practices	3	Political Science	2
Comparative Educational Admin.	3	Principles of Admin.	2
		Social & Economic Devel.	2
Curriculum	2	Sociology of Education	2
Educational Admin. I	3		
Educational Admin. II	3	Thesis	8
Educational Finance	3	Seminar I	1
Educational Planning	3	Seminar II	1
Educational Statistics	2	Seminar III	1
Educational Supervision	2	Seminar IV	1
Group Dynamics	2	Grand Total	48
Methodology of Scientific Research	2		

SOURCE: Division of Education, Universidad del Valle, Cali, 1982.

(master's in rural development extension) offered by Pontificia Universidad Javeriana, in Bogotá. Note in Table 3.13 that such a degree would come out of the *Facultad* of Interdisciplinary Studies, an innovative concept that allows Javeriana to offer combinations of programs to form master's degrees. (See Appendix A for the master's degrees offered by Javeriana.) Table 3.14 shows a curriculum leading to the *Magister en Administración Educacional* (master's in educational administration) from the Universidad del Valle, in Cali. Note that the difference in the number of credits can be explained by the fact that one school is on a semester system, the other on a trimester system.

Master's degree candidates must maintain at least a 3.5 (B) grade average in all graduate courses while in the program, and must write and defend a thesis before the master's degree is awarded. Note the thesis in Tables 3.13 and 3.14. See also Document 3.8, a *Magister en Administración Educacional* (educational administration) from the Universidad del Valle. The document is signed by the *Rector*, Dean, Secretary, and department head of the university.

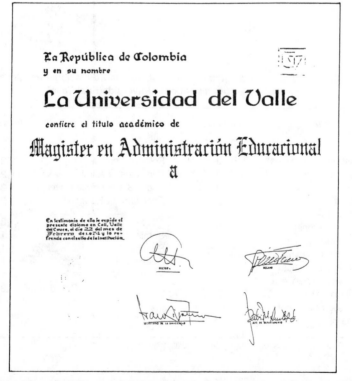

No. 3.8. *Magister en Administración Educacional,* Universidad del Valle.

Doctor (Doctoral) Programs

At the present time, the only university offering the *Doctor* (doctoral) degree is the Pontificia Universidad Javeriana. (See Table 3.12 for graduate programs offered by Javeriana.)

The doctoral programs at Javeriana are designed individually in keeping with the student's aims and prior education; the length of the program varies. However, in order to earn a doctoral degree, the student usually must spend four years in study after the first university degree, and two years after the *Magister*.

Doctoral candidates, who are being prepared to carry out original research, must meet two sets of requirements. They must first, after successfully completing graduate courses and seminars, show a working knowledge of the principles of doing primary research. This includes the following: 1) demonstrable knowledge of basic statistical methods, and 2) competence in one foreign language (usually English, French, or German). Second, candidates must demonstrate competence in the research related to the dissertation by defending it before the graduate faculty. The comprehensive examination for the doctoral is entirely oral.

The Role of the National Council on the Evaluation of Foreign Educational Credentials

The placement recommendations that follow have been approved by the National Council on the Evaluation of Foreign Educational Credentials. In order that these recommendations may be of maximum use to admissions officers, the following information on the development of the terminology used in stating the recommendations, along with instructions for their use, is offered by the Council and the World Education Series Committee.

The recommendations deal with all levels of formal education in roughly chronological order up through the highest degree conferred. Recommendations, as developed through discussion and consensus in the Council, are not directives. Rather, they are general guidelines to help admissions officers determine the admissibility and appropriate level of placement of students from the country under study.

The recommendations should be applied flexibly rather than literally. Before applying the recommendations, admissions officers should read the supporting pages in the text and take into account their own institutional policies and practices. For example, a recommendation may be stated as follows: ". . . may be considered for up to 30 semester hours of transfer credit. . ." The implication is that the U.S. institution may consider giving less than or as much as one year of transfer credit, the decision to be based on various factors—the currentness of the applicant's transfer study, applicability of the study to the U.S. curriculum, quality of grades, and the receiving institution's own policies regarding transfer credit. Similarly, the recommendation ". . . may be considered for freshman admission" indicates possible eligibility only; it is not a recommendation that the candidate be admitted. Although consideration for admission at the same level may be recommended for holders of two different kinds of diplomas, use of identical phrasing in the recommendation does not mean that the two diplomas are identical in nature, quality, or in the quantity of education they represent.

In most cases, the Council will not have attempted to make judgments about the quality of individual schools or types of educational programs within the system under study. Quality clues are provided by the author and must be inferred from a careful reading of the text.

Certain phrases used repeatedly in the recommendations have acquired, within Council usage, specific meanings. For example, "through a course-by-course analysis" means that in dealing with transfer credit, each course taken at the foreign institution is to be judged on an individual basis for its transferability to the receiving institution. Another phrase "where technical training is considered appropriate preparation" suggests that the curriculum followed by the candidate is specialized, and this wording is often a hint that within the foreign system the candidate's educational placement options are limited to certain curriculums. However, while the Council is aware of the educational policies of the country under study, the Council's policies are not necessarily set in conformity with that country's policies. Rather, the recommendations reflect U.S. philosophy and structure of education.

In voting on individual recommendations, Council decisions are made by simple majority. Although consistency among volumes is sought, some differences in philosophy and practice may occur from volume to volume.

Chapter Four

Guidelines and Placement Recommendations

Special Considerations

Colombian Degrees and Diplomas

The higher education degrees and diplomas currently offered in Colombia under Decree 80 are discussed in detail in Chapter Three under "Undergraduate Degrees and Diplomas" and "Graduate Education." Those degrees and diplomas awarded before 1980 are discussed in Chapter Three under "Three-Year Degrees"[1] and "Diplomas—Pre-1980."

Any points of confusion that might arise in regard to terminology usually, but not always, involve the older awards. For example, the title *Experto* was used at both the secondary and the higher education levels in the old system. The secondary *Experto*, which represents nine years of education, is described in Chapter Two under "Curriculums Prior to 1974" and "Documents—Current and Pre-1974." (Also, see Document 2.5.) The *Experto* at the higher education level is described in Chapter Three under "Diplomas—Pre-1980."

Even the generic term *título de* _____ (title of _____) may be somewhat confusing because it appears on documents at all levels of education. Another instance in which usage may be confusing is in regard to the terms *Maestro(a)* and *Maestro(a) Superior*, which under the old system were secondary school diplomas in teacher training. These titles are discussed in Chapter Two. (Also see Documents 2.3 and 2.4.) The term *Maestro* is used in the current system for higher education degrees in the arts that are equivalent to the *Licenciado* (first university degree). These degrees, which are included in the list of degrees or titles considered equivalent to the *Licenciado* (see Chapter Three), include the following: *Maestro en Artes Plásticas* (master of plastic arts); *Maestro en Bellas Artes* (master of fine arts); *Maestro en Cerámica* (master of ceramics); *Maestro en Composición Musical* (master of musical composition); *Maestro en Educación Musical* (master of music education); and *Maestro en Pintura* (master of painting).

Another point of confusion may involve the term *Doctor*. Prior to 1980 it was common for universities to offer first degrees that led to a title of *Doctor*. This was particularly true in law, medicine, and dentistry. One school, Colegio Mayor de Nuestra Señora del Rosario, offered an eight-semester degree in

---

1. Only three first degrees of less than four years' length are offered in Colombia at the present time. See "Three-Year Degrees in Chapter Three."

philosophy that led to the *Doctor en Filosofía*. Any *Doctor* degree offered before 1980 probably is a first university degree that would be considered equivalent to the current eight-semester *Licenciado* or a comparable first university degree.

Also, in one university the *Doctor* degree is still awarded for programs that actually are first degrees. The Universidad Nacional de Colombia/UNC (National University of Colombia) offers the following programs: a 12-semester program in medicine that leads to a *Doctor en Medicina*; a 10-semester program in veterinary medicine leading to a *Doctor en Medicina y Veterinaria*; and a 9-semester program in dentistry that leads to a *Doctor en Odontología*.

At the present time, the only degree offered in Colombia that is considered comparable to the Ph.D. is the *Doctor* offered by Pontificia Universidad Javeriana (Pontifical University of Javeriana), in Bogotá.

Grading Systems

Grading systems in Colombian educational institutions are all mandated by the Ministry of National Education. Grades are usually reported as whole numbers with decimal subdivisions. Admissions officers should be aware that the concept of a D, a passing but unsatisfactory grade, is nonexistent in the Colombian system. It should also be noted that the highest and lowest grades at both the secondary and higher education levels rarely are given.

Grading at the secondary level is based on a scale of 1.0 to 10.0, with 6.0 the lowest passing grade. The suggested equivalencies between U.S. and Colombian systems at the secondary level are described in the section on "Grading at the Secondary Level" in Chapter Two. The grading system prior to 1974 is also described in that section.

At the higher education level, the grading scale is 0.00 to 5.00 with 3.00 the lowest passing grade. See the section on "Grading/Examinations" in Chapter Three for a discussion of grading at the higher education level.

Military and Police Training

Military and police training in Colombia is offered by university-level institutions. Their requirements for admission are the same as those for the universities, with the addition of a physical fitness standard.

The three military institutions are the following: Escuela Militar de Aviación "Marco Fidel Súarez" (Military Aviation School "Marco Fidel Súarez"), in Cali; Escuela Militar de Cadetes (Military Cadet School), in Bogotá; and Escuela Naval de Cadetes "Almirante José Prudencio Padilla" (Naval Cadet School "Admiral José Prudencio Padilla"), on the Island of Manzanillo. These institutions grant first university degrees in economics, engineering, maritime administration, naval engineering, and oceanography.

Police training is offered at the Escuela de Cadetes de Policía "General Santander" (Police Cadet School "General Santander"), in Bogotá. Two programs are offered: an 11-semester program in police administration, leading to a *Licenciado en Estudios Policiales*, and an 8-semester program in police studies leading to the title *Administrador Policial*.

For individual descriptions of military and police training schools, see Section III of Appendix A. Also, see the list of degrees considered comparable to the 8-semester *Licenciado* in Chapter Three.

Transfer of Credits from Colombian Institutions

Undergraduate programs in Colombian universities and other institutions of higher education usually consist of more credit hours per semester than similar programs of study in the United States. No more than 30 semester hours of transfer credit should be granted in the United States for one year of study in Colombia with each course awarded credit on an individual basis.

Graduate programs in Colombian universities resemble those of the United States, and credit is awarded in a similar manner.

Placement Recommendations

Educational Background of Students from Colombia	Placement Recommendations for U.S. Admissions Officers
A. Secondary Credentials	
1. Completed *Ciclo Básico* (basic cycle) of secondary education. (pp. 8–9)	May be placed in grade 10 of secondary school.
2. Holds a *Certificado de Aptitud Profesional*/CAP (certificate of professional aptitude). (p. 27)	Primarily a vocational qualification. Placement should be based on other credentials.
3. Holds a *Certificado de Equivalencia del Grado de Bachiller* (certificate of equivalence to the *Bachiller* diploma). (pp. 27-28, 31)	Primarily a vocational qualification. Placement should be based on other credentials.*
4. Holds a diploma of *Experto* (expert) from a secondary level commercial, industrial, or technical school. (pp. 14, 15, 19, 22, 23)	May be placed in grade 10 of secondary school.
5. Holds a *Bachiller* (secondary school) diploma obtained either on completion of secondary school or by pass-	May be considered for freshman admission. Consideration should be given to the relevance of the student's

---

*For legal purposes in Colombia, this certificate represents the completion of the equivalent of secondary school.

ing the *examen de validación del Bachillerato* (validation exam). (pp. 7, 10-11, 18-19, 30, 31)

academic preparation to the proposed program of study in the United States.

6. Holds a *Maestro(a), Maestro(a) Superior,* or *Normalista Superior* diploma. (pp. 14, 30-31, 65)

May be considered for freshman admission. Consideration should be given to the relevance of the student's academic preparation to the proposed program of study in the United States.

B. Undergraduate Credentials

Students who have completed some coursework for any of the programs listed below may be considered for undergraduate admission with up to a maximum of 30 semester hours of transfer credit for each year, determined through a course-by-course analysis. When length of the program is cited, it refers to the standard length of the program when pursued fulltime. Actual period of attendance may vary.

1. Holds a diploma of *Técnico Profesional Intermedio en*—from a 4- or 5-semester program. (pp. 35-37, 45, 46)

May be considered for undergraduate admission with transfer credit determined through a course-by-course analysis.

2. Holds a diploma of *Tecnólogo* (including the *Regente* in Pharmacy) from a 4- to 7-semester program. (pp. 37, 46-48)

May be considered for undergraduate admission with transfer credit determined through a course-by-course analysis.

3. Holds a postsecondary diploma of *Perito* (2-4 semesters), *Experto* (4-5 semesters), or *Técnico* (6 semesters). (pp. 43-44)

May be considered for undergraduate admission with transfer credit determined through a course-by-course analysis.

4. Holds one of the following 6-semester degrees: *Estadístico, Maestro de Capilla, Licenciado en Enfermería, Lic. en Filosofía, Lic. en Investigación Folklórica.* (p. 43)

May be considered for undergraduate admission with transfer credit determined through a course-by-course analysis.

5. Holds one of the following 7-semester *Licenciado* degrees: *Terapia del Lenguaje, Terapia Física,* or *Terapia Ocupacional.* (p. 43)

May be considered for undergraduate admission with transfer credit determined through a course-by-course analysis.

6. Holds an 8-semester *Licenciado*; or a first university degree including the *Maestro en Artes Plásticas, Maestro en Bellas Artes, Maestro en Cerámica, Maestro en Composición Musical, Maestro en Educación Musical, Maestro en Pintura*; or a comparable degree from a program of 8 or more semesters' duration. (pp. 37-40, 65)

May be considered for graduate admission.

7. Holds a first university degree in dentistry, medicine, pharmacy, or veterinary medicine, including the following: *Dr. en Medicina, Dr. en Medicina y Veterinaria, Dr. en Odontología, Médico, Médico Veterinario, Médico Veterinario y Zootecnista, Médico y Cirujano, Odontólogo, Químico Farmacéutico, Veterinario y Zootecnista.* (pp. 38-40, 66)

May be considered to have the first professional degree in the field; may be considered for graduate admission.

C. Graduate Credentials (pp. 58-63)

---

1. Holds a diploma of *Especialista* from a clinical training program in dentistry, medicine, nursing, veterinary medicine, or other clinically-based programs.

May be considered to have completed a specialized clinical training program.

2. Holds a diploma of *Especialista* from a program which is not clinically-based.

May be considered for graduate admission with transfer credit determined through a course-by-course analysis.

3. Holds a degree of *Magister, Magister Scientiae, Maestría,* or *Master.*

May be considered to have a degree comparable to a master's degree in the U.S.

4. Holds a graduate-level *Doctor* degree.

May be considered to have a degree comparable to an earned doctorate in the same field in the U.S.

D. Seminary Education (pp. 124-125)

---

1. Completed a 3-year program (I-*Ciclo Filosófico*) from a major seminary.

May be considered for undergraduate admission with transfer credit determined through a course-by-course analysis.

2. Completed a 4-year program (II-*Ciclo Teológico*) from a major seminary.

May be considered to have a degree comparable to a Master of Divinity in the U.S.

Appendix A

Colombian Institutions of Higher Education

The following list of institutions of higher education, recognized by the Instituto Colombiano para el Fomento de la Educación Superior/ICFES (Colombian Institute for the Promotion of Higher Education), has been divided into the following three sections according to programs offered:

I. *Formación Intermedia Profesional*/FIP (intermediate professional studies), Level 1 of higher education under Decree 80.

II. *Formación Tecnológica*/FT (technological studies), Level 2 under Decree 80.

III. *Formación Universitaria* (university level studies), Level 3 under Decree 80. In this appendix, the institutions that offer *Formación Avanzada o de Postgrado* (graduate studies), Level 4 of higher education under Decree 80, have been listed in Section III.

In each section the name of the institution is listed alphabetically with, when available, the address, telephone number, enrollment figures for 1981-82, and the status (public or private) of each institution. In Section III, the date of founding, the length of the programs, and the diploma, degree, or title awarded, are also given. In Sections I and II, the length of all programs and the diploma awarded are given at the beginning of the section.

The information in Appendix A was taken from the following sources: Instituto Colombiano para el Fomento de la Educación Superior/ICFES, *Directorio de la Educación Superior en Colombia, 1981*, División de Recursos Bibliográficos (Bogotá, D.E.: División de Publicaciones del ICFES), 1981; ICFES, *Estadísticas de la Educación Superior, 1982*, División de Información Estadística (Bogotá, D.E.: División de Publicaciones del ICFES), 1982; ICFES, "Listado de Universidad y Programas, Modalidad de Formación Avanzada," División de Postgrado, 1983, ICFES. (Xerox)

I. Intermediate Professional Studies (*Formación Intermedia Profesional*)

Length of Program: 4-5 semesters. Title Awarded: *Técnico Profesional Intermedio en*/TPI (intermediate professional technician in).

Institution	Enrollment/Status
Academia de Dibujo Profesional, Avenida 2 Norte No 7-67, Oficinas Ave 9 Norte, No 6-100, Cali. Tel: 601237, 671720, 688784.	864/private
Academia Superior de Artes, Calle 43 No 78-40, Medellín. Tel: 488750, 434851.	885/private
Asociación Colombiana de Recreación, Avenida 32 No 17-30, Bogotá. Tel: 2453047, 2698506.	48/private
Asociación para la Enseñanza (ASPAEN), Calle 69 No 11-36, Bogotá. Tel: 2496846, 2133954.	231/private
Centro Colombiano de Estudios Profesionales, Avenida 2 Norte No 7-67 y Calle 13 Norte No 6N-07, Cali. Tel: 684315, 611833.	1626/private
Centro Colombo Andino, Avenida 19 No 3-16, Oficina 214, Bogotá. Tel: 2827798, 2844006.	612/private
Centro de Carreras Profesionales Intermedias, Avenida 4a No 15-88, Cúcuta. Tel: 25149.	369/private
Centro de Comercio Exterior (CENTROCOMEX), Calle 40A No 13-14, Bogotá. Tel: 2457809.	151/private
Centro de Educación Intermedia Profesional (CEDINPRO), Calle 36 No 5-37, Bogotá. Tel: 2320009.	527/private
Centro de Estudios Artísticos y Técnicos (CEART), Calle 71 No 5-50, Bogotá. Tel: 2350321.	114/private
Centro de Estudios Dirigidos (CED), Calle 21 Norte No 4N-49, Versalles Ave 6 Norte No 22-46, Cali. Tel: 641255, 601603.	281/private
Centro de Investigación Docencia y Consultoría Administrativa (CIDCA), Calle 18 No 8-75, Bogotá. Tel: 2840905, 2830064, 2840925.	2071/private
Centro Latino-Francés (CENLAF), Carrera 16 No 33-80, Oficinas Calle 33A No 15-46, Bogotá. Tel: 2453806, 2450875, 2457322.	42/private
Centro Regional de Educación Superior (CRES), Ave 5 Norte No 22N-27, Cali. Tel: 631400, 685397.	394/private
Centro Superior de Administración Industrial, Calle 14 Norte No 6-26 y Carrera No 8-49, Cali. Tel: 631142, 641816, 801984.	644/private
Centro Superior Profesional, Carrera 4 No 13-23, Ipiales. Tel: 2645.	150/private
Centro Técnico Arquitectónico, Calle 11 No 18-54, Pereira. Tel: 44612.	137/private
Centro Tecnológico de Ingeniería Textil (CIT), Calle 4C No 37-50, Cali. Tel: 582291.	81/private
Centro Universitario de Administración (CENDA), Carrera 13 No 45-67 Piso 2 y Calle 55 No 10-81 Piso 3, Bogotá. Tel: 2459139, 2698626, 2357318.	273/private
Centro Universitario de Administración (CENDA), Cali.	292/private
Centro Universitario de Nuestra Señora de las Mercedes, Calle 73 No 11-92, Bogotá. Tel: 2357239.	207/private
Centro Universitario Nacional de Administración y Hotelería (CUN), Calle 51 No 5-37, Bogotá. Tel: 2451011.	483/private

Colegio Mayor de Nuestra Señora, Carrera 24 No 18-46, Manizales. Tel: 32576, 30337, 31975.	204/private
Colegio Miguel Camacho Perea, Ave 3 Norte No 44-100, Cali. Tel: 682510.	434/private
Colegio Seminario Instituto María Goretti, Plazuela Santiago, Pasto. Tel: 2894, 2314, 4915.	166/private
Colegio Tecnólogo Universitario (UNITEC), Bogotá. *See* Corporación de Educación Superior Intermedia Profesional (UNITEC), Bogotá.	
Corporación de Educación Superior del Trabajo, Calle 20 No 5-30, Bogotá. Tel: 2848012, 2842403.	522/private
Corporación de Educación Superior Intermedia Profesional (UNITEC), Bogotá.	564/private
Corporación Educativa Centro Colombo-Andino, Bogotá.	713/private
Corporación Educativa del Litoral. Escuela de Administración y Mercadotecnia, Carrera 53 No 82-114, Barranquilla. Tel: 353507.	650/private
Corporación Educativa Instituto de Educación Empresarial (IDEE), Ave 1 Norte No 3-27, Cali. Tel: 684722, 611735.	342/private
*Corporación Educativa Superior de Córdoba (CESCO), Carrera 3 No 29-26, Montería. Tel: 4071, 3935, 2467.	513/private
Corporación Instituto de Artes y Ciencias, Calle 58 Carreras 54 y 58, Barranquilla. Tel: 322052.	960/private
Corporación Instituto de Pedagogía Infantil (INPI), Calle 67 No 5-11 y Calle 65 No 5-50, Bogotá. Tel: 2493146, 2110928, 2495475.	358/private
Corporación Instituto Superior de Educación Social (ISES), Calle 33A No 14-29, Bogotá. Tel: 2454434.	46/private
Corporación Internacional para el Desarrollo Educativo (CIDE), Carrera 3 No 74-69/71, Bogotá. Tel: 2499900, 2490968.	253/private
Corporación Universitaria Santa Fé de Bogotá, Carrera 17 No 33-32, Bogotá. Tel: 2453073, 2850963.	414/private
Escuela Colombiana de Carreras Intermedias, Carrera 7 No 53-30, Bogotá. Tel: 2499965.	147/private
Escuela Colombiana de Hotelería y Turismo (ECOTET), Carrera 19 No 100-49, Bogotá.	436/private
Escuela de Administración y Mercadotecnia del Quindío, Ave Bolívar No 3-11, Armenia. Tel: 47809, 49397.	247/private
Escuela de Arte y Diseño de Arquitectura e Ingeniería, Carrera 15 No 34-00, Bogotá. Tel: 2455968.	148/private
Escuela de Artes y Letras, Ave Caracas No 75-59, Bogotá. Tel: 2487218, 2487219, 2592094, 2592115.	298/private
Escuela de Ciencias Económicas y Administrativas (ECEA), Carrera 8 No 45-41, Bogotá. Tel: 2455831.	97/private
Escuela de Diseños Industriales (ACADITEC), Calle 50 No 14-70/76, Bogotá. Tel: 2482856, 2355251.	155/private
Escuela Superior de Administración Agrotécnica y Pedagógica (ESATEP), Calle 66 No 11-28, Bogotá. Tel: 2480119.	107/private
Escuela Superior de Ventas y Mercadotecnia, Ave 2 Norte No 7-67, Cali. Tel: 688784, 688730.	100/private

---

*University level institution offering FIP program.

Escuela Superior Profesional de Carreras Intermedias (INPAHU), Bogotá. *See* Fundación Escuela Superior Profesional (INPAHU), Bogotá.

Fundación Escuela Superior Profesional (INPAHU), Ave 39 No 15-58, Bogotá. Tel: 2453652, 2855314, 2857085.	2370/private
Fundación Instituto de Enseñanza Profesional (INESPRO), Carrera 6 No 47-38, Bogotá. Tel: 2856992, 2853797.	341/private
Fundación Instituto de Investigación de la Expresión Colombiana (IDEC), Carrera 9 No 11-36, Chía. Tel: 98533-425.	76/private
Fundación Interamericana Técnica (FIT), Bogotá.	NA/private
Fundación para el Desarrollo de las Ciencias de la Comunicación Social (FUNDEMOS), Calle 61 No 3B-62 y 4-06, Bogotá. Tel: 2496024, 2110694.	391/private
Instituto Colombiano de Telecomunicaciones y Electrónica, Carrera 7 No 44-76, Bogotá. Tel: 2852048, 2858285.	308/private
Instituto de Administración y Finanzas (IAF), Carrera 7 No 23-15, Pereira. Tel: 49000, 37848.	434/private
Instituto de Administración y Finanzas de Cartagena (IAFIC), Calle Santa Teresa No 32-25, Cartagena. Tel: 41748.	1750/private
Instituto de Artes, Carrera 42 No 50A-12, Medellín. Tel: 395492, 393947.	354/private
Instituto de Carreras Intermedias (IDCI), Cali.	659/private
Instituto de Ciencias Sociales, Carrera 7A No 23-74, Cali. Tel: 701415, 811671.	209/public
Instituto de Educación Intermedia Profesional de Roldanillo, Roldanillo.	266/public
Instituto de Educación Intermedia Profesional de San Juan del Cesar, Apartado Aéreo 438, San Juan del Cesar.	131/public

Instituto de Enseñanza Profesional (INESPRO), Bogotá. *See* Fundación Instituto de Enseñanza Profesional (INESPRO), Bogotá.

Instituto de Incorporación Universitaria (INUNIVERSITAS), Calle 82 No 11-41 y 12-15, Carrera 13 No 83-21, Bogotá. Tel: 2366846.	897/private

Instituto de Pedagogía Infantil (INPI), Bogotá. *See* Corporación Instituto de Pedagogía Infantil (INPI), Bogotá.

Instituto Grancolombiano de Carreras Intermedias (CIDE), Calle 42 No 27-28, Bucaramanga. Tel: 56662, 57822.	117/private
Instituto Meyer, Calle 17 No 10-16 Piso 2, Carrera 13 No 62-40, Carrera 9 No 23-35, Bogotá. Tel: 2814215, 2814395, 2489168, 2833902.	33/private
Instituto Nacional de Capacitación Empresarial (INCE), Urbanización ACOPI, Manzana 15 Menga, Cali.	265/private
Instituto Nacional de Formación Intermedia Profesional de San Andrés, San Andrés.	122/public
Instituto Superior de Carreras Técnicas (INSUTEC), Ave 39 No 13-49, Bogotá. Tel: 2859405, 2859063.	142/private

Instituto Superior de Educación Social (ISES), Bogotá. *See* Corporación Instituto Superior de Educación Social (ISES), Bogotá.

Instituto Técnico Agrícola (ITA), Buga.	8/public
Instituto Técnico Central, Calle 13 No 16-74, Bogotá. Tel: 2416028, 2827226.	433/public
Instituto Técnico Nacional de Comercio "Simón Rodríguez," Carrera 1D Bis No 49-20, Cali. Tel: 411218, 411179.	250/public
Instituto Técnico Profesional "Julio Duque Baena," Bogotá.	64/private
Instituto Técnico Superior Universitario (UNIVERSITEC), Calle 71A No 5-47, Bogotá. Tel: 2493603.	604/private

Instituto Tecnológico de Educación Superior (ITECS), Carrera 25 No 5-80,   351/private
   Cali. Tel: 531553, 586070, 511502.

Instituto Tolimense de Formación Intermedia Profesional (ITFIP), Espinal.   136/public

Taller Cinco Centro de Diseño, Bogotá.   192/private

Unidad de Carreras Intermedias del Cauca (UCICA), Carrera 7 No 6-10   583/private
   (Oficinas) y Carrera 7 No 5-61 (Aulas), Popayán.

Unidad de Carreras Intermedias de Sevilla (UCIS), Sevilla.   124/public

II. Technological Studies (*Formación Tecnológica*)

Length of Program: 4-7 semesters. Title Awarded: *Tecnólogo en* (technologist in).

Institution	Enrollment/Status
Centro de Investigaciones y Planeamiento Administrativo (CEIPA), Medellín.	1059/private
Centro de Investigaciones y Recreación Dirigida (CIRDI), Calle 69 No 7-77, Bogotá. Tel: 2494508.	68/private
Centro Universitario del Norte del Valle, Calle 10 No 3-95, Apartado Aéreo 18, Cartago. Tel: 5237.	235/private
*Colegio Mayor de Antioquia, Calle 65 No 78 Robledo, Apartado Aéreo 5177, Medellín. Tel: 344335.	578/public
Colegio Mayor de Cultura de Bolívar, Calle de la Factoría, No 36-101, Cartagena. Tel: 44060, 42484, 42486.	800/public
Colegio Mayor de Cultura Popular del Cauca, Calle 5 No 4-33, Popayán. Tel: 1109.	61/public
*Colegio Mayor de Cundinamarca, Calle 28 No 6-02, Bogotá. Tel: 2456737, 2340257.	1572/public
*Colegio Mayor de Nuestra Señora del Rosario, Calle 14 No 6-25, Bogotá. Tel: 2820088, 2410367.	2917/private
Corporación Centro Educacional de Cómputos y Sistemas (CEDESISTEMAS), Calle 49 No 43-52, Apartado Aéreo 223, Medellín. Tel: 392256, 396739, 390872.	360/private
Corporación de Educación del Norte de Tolima (COREDUCACION), Honda.	156/private
Corporación Educativa Centro Superior de Cali, Calle 14 Norte No 6-26 y Carrera 6 No 8-49, Apartado Aéreo 5386, Cali. Tel: 641518, 641816, 631142, 801984.	287/private
Corporación Educativa Escuela Superior de Mercadotecnia (ESUMER), Calle 76 No 80-196 Carretera al Mar, Medellín. Tel: 347816, 342288, 344259.	457/private
Corporación Educativa Instituto de Educación Empresarial (IDEE), Ave 1 Norte No 3-27, Cali. Tel: 684722, 611735.	431/private
Corporación Escuela de Administración de Empresas (EAE), Calle 2A No 24C-95, Apartado Aéreo 2144, Cali. Tel: 588107.	505/private
Corporación Escuela Tributaria de Colombia, Calle 55 No 41-10, Apartado Aéreo 4800, Medellín. Tel: 399500, 399089.	426/private
*Corporación Universitaria de Ibagué (CORUNIVERSITARIA), Ibagué.	651/private

---

*University level institution offering FT program.

Fundación Escuela Colombiana de Mercadotecnia, Calle 50 No 40-39, Apartado Aéreo 4983, Medellín. Tel: 399720, 393827.	388/private
*Fundación Instituto de Ciencias de la Salud (CES), Transversal Superior X Calle 10 Variante Las Palmas, Apartado Aéreo 0549591, Medellín. Tel: 462504, 410073.	733/private
Fundación Politécnico Grancolombiano, Calle 57 Carrera 3 Este, Apartado Aéreo 90853, Bogotá. Tel: 2570860, 2562891.	1109/private
*Fundación Universidad Central, Carrera 16 No 24-45, Bogotá. Tel: 2341966, 2415181, 2346229, 2838309.	4510/private
*Fundación Universidad Escuela de Administración y Finanzas y Tecnologías (EAFIT), Carrera 49 No 7-50, Apartado Aéreo 3300, Medellín. Tel: 550500, 552891.	2942/private
*Fundación Universidad de Bogotá "Jorge Tadeo Lozano," Calle 23 No 4-47, Apartado Aéreo 34185, Bogotá. Tel: Conm. 2412287, 2434932, 2434934, 2834750/30.	6631/private
*Fundación Universidad de Bogotá "Jorge Tadeo Lozano"—Cartagena, Carrera 4 No 38-40, Apartado Aéreo 1310, Cartagena. Tel: 42314, 42417.	806/private
*Fundación Universidad de la Sabana, Calle 70 No 11-79, Bogotá. Tel: 2496846, 2494507, 2490385, 2496862, 2496830.	1959/private
*Fundación Universidad del Norte, Kt 5 Carretera a Pto. Colombia, Apartado Postal 0809, Barranquilla. Tel: Conm. 57720, 46741.	2898/private
*Instituto de Ciencias de la Salud, Medellín. *See* Fundación Instituto de Ciencias de la Salud (CES), Medellín.	
Instituto Politécnico de Electrónica y Comunicaciones (IPEC), Transversal 49 No 105-84, Bogotá. Tel: 2533277, 2532065.	20/public
Instituto Superior de Ciencias Sociales y Económico Familiares (ICSEF), Calle 34 No 6-56, Bogotá. Tel: 2454696.	105/private
Instituto Superior de Educación Rural (ISER), Apartado Aéreo 1031, Pamplona. Tel: 2597.	102/public
Instituto Superior de Historia de Colombia, Carrera 9 No 9-52, Bogotá. Tel: 2825316, 2825356.	100/private
Instituto Técnico Superior "Pascual Bravo," Carretera al Volador Robledo, Medellín. Tel: 341014, 345082.	743/public
*Instituto Técnico Universitario de Cundinamarca (ITUC), Apartado Aéreo 3033, Fusagasugá. Tel: 2144.	723/public
*Instituto Técnico Universitario de Cundinamarca (ITUC), Carrera 15 Calle 16, Girardot. Tel: 6205.	290/public
*Instituto Técnico Universitario de Cundinamarca (ITUC), Calle 6 No 9-80, Ubaté. Tel: 3055, 3056.	297/public
Instituto Tecnológico de Administración y Economía (ITAE), Calle 35 No 9-81, Apartado Aéreo 2147, Bucaramanga. Tel: 27145.	436/private
Instituto Tecnológico de Electrónica y Comunicaciones (ITEC), Bogotá.	–/public
Instituto Tecnológico Santandereano (ITS), Calle 10 No 28-77, Apartado Aéreo 899, Bucaramanga. Tel: 55148, 58366.	618/public
Politécnico Colombiano "Jaime Isaza Cadavid," Ave Las Vegas Calle 10, Apartado Aéreo 4932, El Poblado, Medellín. Tel: 460920.	3145/public

---

*University level institution offering FT program.

Politécnico Colombiano "Jaime Isaza Cadavid," Rionegro.	145/public
*Universidad Autónoma del Caribe, Carrera 46 No 88-26, Apartado Aéreo 50826, Barranquilla. Tel: 350826, 355804.	1967/public
*Universidad Católica de Manizales, Carrera 23 No 60-63 Zona 4, Apartado Aéreo 357, Manizales. Tel: 51412, 53121, 55470.	1152/private
*Universidad de Antioquia, Ciudad Universitaria, Apartado Aéreo 1226, Medellín. Tel: 330599, 334141.	15,732/public
*Universidad de Córdoba, Carretera a Cereté Km 5, Apartado Aéreo 354, Montería. Tel: 8499, 4600, 3278, Conm. 3381.	2893/public
*Universidad del Cauca, Calle 5 No 4-70, Popayán. Tel: 1893, 3020, 4115.	2859/public
*Universidad del Quindío, Carrera 15 Calle 12, Apartado Aéreo 460, Armenia. Tel: 49341, 41501.	4828/public
*Universidad del Tolima, Santa Helena, Apartado Aéreo 546, Ibagué. Tel: 32544, 34219, 34224, 32733.	4082/public
*Universidad del Valle, Barrio San Bernardo, Apartado Aéreo 2188, Cali. Tel: 392207, 392310, 391486.	7061/public
*Universidad de Sucre, Calle 19 No 22-58, Apartado Aéreo 406, Sincelejo.	344/public
*Universidad Distrital "Francisco José de Caldas," Carrera 8a No 40-78, Apartado Aéreo 8668, Bogotá. Tel: 2457088, 2450440.	3239/public
*Universidad Francisco de Paula Santander—Bochalema, Bochalema (N. de S.).	101/public
*Universidad Francisco de Paula Santander, Avenida Gran Colombia No 12E-96, Cúcuta. Tel: 21371, 40072, 44253.	3265/public
*Universidad Francisco de Paula Santander, Ocaña, Tel: 3344, 2222, 2271.	236/public
*Universidad Industrial de Santander, Ciudad Universitaria, Apartado Aéreo 678, Bucaramanga. Tel: Conm. 56141-49.	4831/public
*Universidad Nacional de Colombia-Medellín, Autopista Robledo Carretera al Mar, Medellín. Tel: 300540, 300111.	4814/public
*Universidad Pontificia Bolivariana, Calle 52 No 40-88, Apartado Aéreo 1178, Medellín. Tel: 497199 Conm. 430300.	4605/private
*Universidad Social Católica de La Salle, Calle 11 No 1-47, Bogotá. Tel: 2346137, 2830900, 2825696.	7357/private
*Universidad Surcolombiana, Calle 9 No 7-82, Apartado Aéreo 385, Neiva. Tel: 27266, 27277.	1950/public
*Universidad Tecnológica del Chocó "Diego Luis Córdoba," Carrera 2 No 25-22, Apartado Aéreo 22, Quibdó. Tel: 735, 589.	1957/public
*Universidad Tecnológica de los Llanos Orientales, Kilómetro 11 Vía Puerto López, Apartado Aéreo 2621, Villavicencio. Tel: 3449, 6200, 3484, 6828, 3909.	836/public
*Universidad Tecnológica de Pereira, Apartado Aéreo 97, Pereira. Tel: 32781, 34944.	3258/public

---

*University level institution offering FT program.

III. University Level Studies (*Formación Universitaria*) and Graduate Study (*Formación Avanzada o de Postgrado*)

This section also includes the founding dates for the public (*oficiales*) and private (*no oficiales*) universities and other institutions of higher education and further identifies each university by type: national (*nacional*), state (*departamental*), or municipal (*municipal*). Information on the status of each university (e.g., public/national, or private) is given in parentheses following the background information. Branch campuses (*seccionales*) and their programs follow the listing of the main campus; the names of the branch campuses are not boldfaced.

Undergraduate level programs are alphabetized in English with the specific degree or title awarded given in Spanish. Graduate level programs of *Especialista, Maestría,* and *Doctor* are listed alphabetically in Spanish with the degree or title awarded noted in the heading. The length of undergraduate programs is given in semesters. Degrees and titles are abbreviated as follows: *Doctor en, Dr. en.; Ingeniero, Ing.; Licenciado en, Lic. en.; Técnico Profesional Intermedio, TPI; Tecnólogo en, Tgo. en.* NA indicates information was not available.

An asterisk (*) beside a program points to a technological studies (FT) program; the dagger (†) to an intermediate professional studies (FIP) program. The double dagger (‡) indicates that the program was not accepting new students in 1980 and probably will be cancelled; the number sign (#) shows that the program is 4 semesters in length, after which the student must transfer to another institution to complete the program of study. The section mark (§) points to a 3-semester program that enables students with the title of *Tecnólogo* to earn a *Licenciado.* The parallels symbol (‖) indicates the program is taken by correspondence.

Centro Universitario Militar Nueva Granada
Calle 81 Carrera 38, Bogotá.
Tel: 2507923.
Enrollment: 1641. (public)

Undergraduate Program of Study	Length	Title Awarded
Medicine	12	*Médico*

Colegio Mayor de Antioquia
Calle 65 No. 78 Robledo, Apartado Aéreo 5177, Medellín.
Tel: 344335. Established 1945.
Enrollment: 578. (public)

Undergraduate Programs of Study	Length	Title Awarded
Architectural Drafting & Engineering Technology*	6	*Tgo. en Delineante de Arquitectura e Ingeniería*
Bacteriology & Clinical Laboratory	8	*Bacteriólogo y Laboratorista Clínico*
Bilingual Secretarial Technology*	6	*Tgo. en Secretariado Bilingüe*
Social Welfare Technology*	6	NA
Tourism Administration Technology*	6	*Tgo. en Administración Turística*

Colegio Mayor de Cundinamarca
Calle 28 No. 6-02, Bogotá.
Tel: 2456737, 2340257. Established 1945.
Enrollment: 1572. (public)

Undergraduate Programs of Study	Length	Title Awarded
Architectural Drafting & Engineering Technology*	6	*Tgo. en Delineante de Arquitectura e Ingeniería*
Bacteriology & Clinical Laboratory	8	*Bacterióloga y Laboratorista Clínica*
Commercial Bilingual Education Technology*	6	*Tgo. en Comercio e Idiomas*
Social Work‡	8	*Trabajadora Social*

Colegio Mayor de Nuestra Señora del Rosario
Calle 14 No. 6-25, Bogotá.
Tel: 2820088, 2410367. Established 1653.
Enrollment: 2375. (private)

Undergraduate Programs of Study	Length	Title Awarded
Business Administration	10	*Administrador de Empresas*
Economics	10	*Economista*
Law	10	*Abogado*
Medicine	10	*Médico*
Nursing	8	*Enfermero*
Occupational Therapy	8	*Terapeuta Ocupacional*
Philosophy & Letters	8	*Filósofo o Diplomado en Filosofía y Letras*
Phonoaudiology	8	*Fonoaudiólogo*
Physical Therapy	8	*Fisioterapeuta*
Translation & Interpretation Technology*	8	*Tgo. en Traducción* or *Tgo. en Interpretación Consecutiva y/o Simultánea*

Specialist Programs of Study. Title Awarded—*Especialista en . . . Administración de Empresas; Anestesiología; Cardiología; Cirugía Cardiomuscular; Cirugía General; Cirugía Plástica; Cirugía Toráxica; Derecho Administrativo; Derecho Comercial; Derecho Financiero; Derecho Procesal; Derecho Tributario; Economía y Comercialización Internacional; Finanzas Privadas; Ginecología; Marketing; Medicina Física y Rehabilitación; Medicina Interna; Neurocirugía; Neurología; Ortopedia; Otorrinolaringología; Patología; Pediatría; Psiquiatría; Radiología; Urología.*

Colegio Odontológico Colombiano
Bogotá.
See Fundación Colegio Odontológico Colombiano, Bogotá.

Colegio Tecnológico Universitario (UNITEC)
Bogotá.
See Corporación de Educación Superior Intermedia Profesional (UNITEC), Bogotá.

Corporación Autónoma de Occidente
Apartado Aéreo 2790, Cali.
Tel: 585060, 511653.
Enrollment: 1519. (private)

Undergraduate Programs of Study	Length	Title Awarded
Economics	12	*Economista*
Electrical Engineering	12	*Ing. Eléctrico*
Industrial Engineering	12	*Ing. Industrial*
Mechanical Engineering	12	*Ing. Mecánico*

Corporación Autónoma Universitaria de Manizales
Apartado Aéreo 441, Manizales.
Tel: 25807.
Enrollment: 181. (private)

Undergraduate Program of Study	Length	Title Awarded
Dentistry	10	*Odontólogo*

Corporación de Educación Superior de Boyacá
Tunja.
Enrollment: 80. (private)
No further information available.

Corporación de Estudios Superiores Universidad Independiente de Colombia "Antonio Nariño"
Calle 20 Sur No. 13-61, Bogotá.
Tel: 2394198.
Enrollment: 1042. (private)

Undergraduate Programs of Study	Length	Degree or Title Awarded
Accounting, Public	10	*Contador Público*
Business Administration	10	*Administrador de Empresas*
Education: Chemistry & Biology	8	*Lic. en Química y Biología*
Dance & Theatre	8	*Lic. en Danzas y Teatro*
Mathematics & Physics	8	*Lic. en Matemáticas y Física*
Social Sciences	8	*Lic. en Ciencias Sociales*

Corporación Educativa Mayor del Desarrollo "Simón Bolívar"
Calle 68 No. 54-82, Apartado Aéreo 15595, Barranquilla.
Tel: 329178. Established 1972.
Enrollment: 3377. (private)

Undergraduate Programs of Study	Length	Degree or Title Awarded
Economics	10	*Economista*

Education: Social Sciences	9	*Lic. en Ciencias Sociales*
Law	10	*Abogado*
Social Work	8	*Trabajador Social*
Sociology	10	*Sociólogo*

Corporación Educativa Superior de Córdoba (CESCO)
Carrera 3 No. 29-26, Montería.
Tel: 4071, 3935, 2467.
Enrollment: 513. (private)

Undergraduate Programs of Study	Length	Title Awarded
Business Administration†	5	*TPI en Administración de Empresas*
Educational Administration†	5	*TPI en Administración Educativa*
Languages†	5	*TPI en Idiomas*
Law	10	*Abogado*
Social Work†	5	*TPI en Trabajo Social*

Corporación Escuela de Ciencias de la Salud de la Sociedad de Cirugía de Bogotá
Calle 10 No. 18-75 Piso 2, Bogotá.
Tel: 2775787, 2475413, 2775716. Established 1976.
Enrollment: 221. (private)

Undergraduate Program of Study	Length	Title Awarded
Nursing	8	*Enfermera*

Corporación Instituto Caldas
Calle 48 No. 39-234, Apartado Aéreo 1642, Bucaramanga.
Tel: 75161, 75111. Established 1955.
Enrollment: 2012. (private)

Undergraduate Programs of Study	Length	Title Awarded
Accounting, Public	11	*Contador Público*
Education: Preschool Educational Technology*	6	*Tgo. en Educación Pre-escolar*
Financial Administration	11	*Administrador de Empresas*
Law	11	*Abogado*

Corporación Instituto Colombiano de Estudios Superiores de Incolda (ICESI)
Carrera 9a. No. 9-49, Piso 2, Cali.
Tel: 791723, 821093, 871989, 821748.
Enrollment: 238. (private)

Undergraduate Program of Study	Length	Title Awarded
Business Administration	10	*Administrador de Empresas*

Corporación Instituto Docente de la Cooperativa para el Fomento de la Educación Superior (COOFES)
Carrera 9a. No. 19-03, Apartado Aéreo 868, Manizales.
Tel: 27450, 26988, 32682, 22558. Established 1972.
Enrollment: 1942. (private)

Undergraduate Programs of Study	Length	Title Awarded
Accounting, Public	11	*Contador Público*
Economics	10	*Economista*
Law	11	*Abogado*
Psychology	10	*Psicólogo*

Corporación Metropolitana para la Educación Superior
Carrera 42F No. 75B-169, Apartado Aéreo 50576, Barranquilla.
Tel: 353757, 350120. Established 1973.
Enrollment: 3092. (private)

Undergraduate Programs of Study	Length	Title Awarded
Bacteriology	8	*Bacteriólogo*
Medicine	12	*Médico y Cirujano*
Nursing	8	*Enfermero*
Nutrition & Dietetics	8	*Nutricionista y Dietista*
Philosophy & Letters	8	*Profesor en Filosofía y Letras*
Psychology	10	*Psicólogo*
Social Work	8	*Trabajador Social*

Corporación Tecnológica de Bolívar
Carrera 21 No. 25-92, Apartado Aéreo 1372, Cartagena.
Tel: 40975, 47429. Established 1970.
Enrollment: 1200. (private)

Undergraduate Programs of Study	Length	Title Awarded
Economics	10	*Economista*
Electrical Engineering	10	*Ing. Eléctrico*
Industrial Engineering	10	*Ing. Industrial*
Mechanical Engineering	10	*Ing. Mecánico*

Corporación Unicosta
Carreras 54 y 58 Calle 58, Apartado Aéreo 50366, Barranquilla.
Tel: 328540 al 328544. Established 1966.
Enrollment: 4076. (private)

Undergraduate Programs of Study	Length	Degree or Title Awarded
Architecture	10	*Arquitecto*
Business Administration	10	*Administrador de Empresas*
Civil Engineering	10	*Ing. Civil*

Economics	10	*Economista*
Education:		
Educational Administration‡	8	NA
Educational Psychology	8	*Lic. en Psicopedagogía*
Mathematics & Physics	8	*Lic. en Matemáticas y Física*
Modern Languages	8	*Lic. en Lenguas Modernas*
Orientation & Counseling‡	8	*Lic. en Orientación y Consejería*
Physical Education	8	*Lic. en Educación Física*
Law	10-12	*Abogado*

Corporación Universidad Autónoma del Caribe
Barranquilla.
See Universidad Autónoma del Caribe, Barranquilla.

Corporación Universidad de Medellín
Medellín.
See Universidad de Medellín, Medellín.

Corporación Universidad La Gran Colombia
Bogotá.
See Universidad La Gran Colombia, Bogotá.

Corporación Universidad Libre de Colombia
Carrera 6 No. 8-06, Bogotá.
Tel: 2344883, 2344884. Established 1955.
Enrollment: 5410. (private)

Undergraduate Programs of Study	Length	Degree or Title Awarded
Accounting, Public	10	*Contador Público*
Education: Biological Sciences	8	*Lic. en Ciencias Biológicas*
Chemistry	8	*Lic. en Química*
Languages	8	*Lic. en Idiomas*
Mathematics	8	*Lic. en Matemáticas*
Physics	8	*Lic. en Física*
Social Sciences	8	*Lic. en Ciencias Sociales*
Industrial Engineering‡	10	*Ing. Industrial*
Law	10-12	*Abogado*
Metallurgical Engineering	10	*Ing. Metalúrgico*

Seccionales (Branch Campuses)

Corporación Universidad Libre de Colombia-Barranquilla
Calle 66 No. 50-52, Barranquilla.
Tel: 369088.
Enrollment: 2363.

Undergraduate Program of Study	Length	Title Awarded
Law	10	*Abogado*

Corporación Universidad Libre de Colombia-Cali
Ave 2 No. 13N-147, Apartado Aéreo 1040, Cali.
Tel: 686571.
Enrollment: 4222.

Undergraduate Programs of Study	Length	Title Awarded
Accounting, Public	10	*Contador Público*
Business Administration	10	*Administrador de Empresas*
Law	10-12	*Abogado*
Medicine	10	*Médico*

Corporación Universidad Libre de Colombia-Cúcuta
Ave 4a. No. 13-50, Cúcuta.
Tel: 23541, 23723, 21004.
Enrollment: 1079.

Undergraduate Programs of Study	Length	Title Awarded
Accounting, Public	10	*Contador Público*
Law	10-12	*Abogado*

Corporación Universidad Libre de Colombia-Pereira
Carrera 7 No. 40-03, Apartado Aéreo 1330, Pereira.
Tel: 37766, 34218, 34217.
Enrollment: 1759.

Undergraduate Programs of Study	Length	Title Awarded
Economics	10	*Economista*
Law	10-12	*Abogado*

Corporación Universidad Libre de Colombia-Socorro
Calle 16 No. 14-08, Socorro.
Tel: 2240.
Enrollment: 388.

Undergraduate Programs of Study	Length	Degree Awarded
Education: Philology & Languages	8	*Lic. en Filología e Idiomas*
Physics & Mathematics	8	*Lic. en Física y Matemáticas*
Social Sciences	8	*Lic. en Ciencias Sociales*

Corporación Universidad Piloto de Colombia
Carrera 9 No. 45A-44, Apartado Aéreo 053658, Bogotá.
Tel: 2458498, 2457398, 2459036. Established 1962.
Enrollment: 2061. (private)

Undergraduate Programs of Study	Length	Title Awarded
Architecture	10	*Arquitecto*
Economics	10	*Economista*
Systems Engineering	10	*Ing. de Sistemas*

Corporación Universitaria Autónoma de Bucaramanga (UNAB)
Bucaramanga.
Enrollment: 2098. (private)
No further information available.

Corporación Universitaria de Ibagué (CORUNIVERSITARIA)
Ibagué.
Enrollment: 651. (private)

Undergraduate Programs of Study	Length	Title Awarded
Accounting Technology*	6	*Tgo. en Contabilidad*
Financial Administration	10	*Administrador de Financiera*
Industrial Technology*	6	*Tgo. en Tecnología Industrial*
Market & Sales Techology*	6	*Tgo. en Mercado y Ventas*

Escuela Colombiana de Ingeniería "Julio Garavito"
Carrera 6 No. 118-60, Apartado Aéreo 14520, Bogotá.
Tel: 2133978, 2134650. Established 1972.
Enrollment: 866. (private)

Undergraduate Programs of Study	Length	Title Awarded
Civil Engineering	10	*Ing. Civil*
Electrical Engineering	10	*Ing. Electricista*

Escuela de Administración de Negocios (EAN)
Calle 72 No. 9-71, Apartado Aéreo 100888, Bogotá.
Tel: 2112932. Established 1968.
Enrollment: 1507. (private)

Undergraduate Program of Study	Length	Title Awarded
Business Administration	10	*Administrador de Empresas*

Escuela de Cadetes de Policía "General Santander"
Autopista Sur, Calle 42, Bogotá.
Tel: 2305801, 2305711. Established 1940.
Enrollment: 506. (public/national)

Undergraduate Programs of Study	Length	Degree or Title Awarded
Police Administration	11	*Lic. en Estudios Policiales*
Police Studies	8	*Administrador Policial*

Escuela de Ingeniería de Antioquia
Calle 25 Sur No. 42-73, Apartado Aéreo 7516, Medellín.
Tel: 764539, 764360.
Enrollment: 148. (private)

Undergraduate Program of Study	Length	Title Awarded
Civil Engineering	10	*Ing. Civil*

Escuela Militar de Aviación "Marco Fidel Suárez"
Carrera 8a. No. 58-67, Cali.
Tel: 491021, 491727, 491716. Established 1960.
Enrollment: 370. (public/national)

Undergraduate Program of Study	Length	Title Awarded
Aeronautic Administration	8	*Administrador Aeronáutica*

Escuela Militar de Cadetes
Calle 81 Carrera 38, Bogotá.
Tel: 2406080.
Enrollment: 551. (public/national)

Undergraduate Programs of Study	Length	Title Awarded
Economics	10	*Economista*
Civil Engineering	10	*Ing. Civil*

Escuela Naval de Cadetes "Almirante José Prudencio Padilla"
Isla de Manzanillo, Cartagena.
Tel: 20978, 22133. Established 1822.
Enrollment: 397. (public/national)

Undergraduate Programs of Study	Length	Title Awarded
Maritime Administration	10	*Administrador Marítimo*
Naval Engineering	10	*Ing. Naval*
Physical Oceanography	10	*Oceanógrafo Físico*

Escuela Superior de Administración Pública (ESAP)
Diagonal 40 No. 46A-37, Apartado Aéreo 29745, Bogotá.
Tel: 2699406, 2699306. Established 1958.
Enrollment: 727. (public/national)

Undergraduate Program of Study	Length	Title Awarded
Administrative & Political Sciences	10	*Administrador Público*

Specialist Programs of Study. Titles Awarded—*Especialista en* . . . *Administración de la Planeación Urbana y Regional; Administración Pública; Finanzas Públicas; Proyectos de Desarrollo.*

Fundación Colegio de Estudios Superiores de Administración (CESA)
Diagonal 35 No. 5-41, Bogotá.
Tel: 2453908, 2326060. Established 1974.
Enrollment 241. (private)

Undergraduate Program of Study	Length	Title Awarded
Business Administration	9	*Administrador de Empresas*

Fundación Colegio Odontológico Colombiano
Calle 13 No 4-38, Apartado Aéreo 34196, Bogotá.
Tel: 3421375. Established 1974.
Enrollment: 2732. (private)

Undergraduate Program of Study	Length	Title Awarded
Dentistry	10	*Odontólogo*

Fundación Educacional Autónoma de Colombia (FEAC)
Carrera 5 No. 11-43, Apartado Aéreo 1998, Bogotá.
Tel: 2421847, 2423781, 2343179, 2832638. Established 1971.
Enrollment: 2834. (private)

Undergraduate Programs of Study	Length	Title Awarded
Economics	10	*Economista*
Industrial Engineering	10	*Ing. Industrial*
Law	10	*Abogado*
Systems Engineering	10	*Ing. de Sistemas*

Fundación Educacional Interamericana
Diagonal 47 No. 15-50, Bogotá.
Tel: 2853830, 2698328, 2452239. Established 1970.
Enrollment: 5377. (private)

Undergraduate Programs of Study	Length	Title Awarded
Architecture	11	*Arquitecto*
Civil Engineering	12	*Ing. Civil*
Economics	10	*Economista*
Industrial Engineering	12	*Ing. Industrial*
Law	10	*Abogado*
Psychology	10	*Psicólogo*

Fundación Escuela Colombiana de Medicina
Calle 134 No. 13-81, Bogotá.
Tel: 2581749.
Enrollment: 416. (private)

Undergraduate Program of Study	Length	Title Awarded
Medicine	12	*Médico*

Specialist Program of Study. Title Awarded—*Especialista en . . . Psiquiatría.*

Fundación Escuela de Medicina "Juan N. Corpas"
Ave Flores de los Andes, Suba Km. 3, Bogotá.
Tel: 2543085, 2543540, 2543550, 2545612. Established 1972.
Enrollment: 1219. (private)

Undergraduate Program of Study	Length	Title Awarded
Medicine	12	*Médico*

Fundación Instituto de Ciencias de la Salud (CES)
Transversal Superior X Calle 10 Variante Las Palmas,
  Apartado Aéreo 054591, Medellín.
Tel: 462504, 510073.
Enrollment: 733. (private)

Undergraduate Programs of Study	Length	Title Awarded
Dentistry	10	*Odontólogo*
Medicine	12	*Médico*
Nursing Technology*	6	*Tgo. en Enfermería*

Specialist Programs of Study. Title Awarded—*Especialista en . . . Odontopediatría Clínica; Ortodoncia Preventiva (Estomatología Pediátrica).*

Fundación Instituto Universitario de Ciencias y Tecnologías "Konrad Lorenz"
Bogotá.
Enrollment: 60. (private)

Fundación Universidad Autónoma de Colombia (FEAC)
Bogotá.
See Fundación Educacional Autónoma de Colombia (FEAC), Bogotá.

Fundación Universidad Central
Carrera 16 No. 24-45, Bogotá.
Tel: 2341966, 2415181, 2346229, 2838309.
Enrollment: 4816. (private)

Undergraduate Programs of Study	Length	Title Awarded
Accounting, Public	10	*Contador Público*
Advertising & Commercialization	6	*Tgo. en Publicidad y*
Technology*		*Comercialización*
Business Administration	10	*Administrador de Empresas*
Economics	10	*Economista*

Master's Program of Study. Title Awarded—*Magister en Ciencias Financieras y de Sistemas.*

**Fundación Universidad Escuela de Administración
y Finanzas y Tecnologías (EAFIT)**
Carrera 49 No. 7-50, Apartado Aéreo 3300, Medellín.
Tel: 550500, 552891. Established 1960.
Enrollment: 2942. (private)

Undergraduate Programs of Study	Length	Title Awarded
Accounting, Public	10	*Contador Público*
Business Administration	10-12	*Administrador de Empresas*
Production Engineering	10	*Ing. de Producción*
Systems Engineering	11	*Ing. de Sistemas*

Specialist Programs of Study. Title Awarded—*Especialista en . . . Administración Agropecuaria; Economía; Finanzas; Instituciones Financieras; Mercadeo; Mercadeo Internacional; Relaciones Industriales; Sistemas de Información Administrativa.*

Master's Program of Study. Title Awarded—*Magister en . . . Administración; Matemáticas Aplicadas.*

Fundación Universidad de América
Calle 77 No. 13-47, Bogotá.
Tel: 2578901, 2485405, 2359012. Established 1952.
Enrollment: 2300. (private)

Undergraduate Programs of Study	Length	Title Awarded
Architecture	10	*Arquitecto*
Chemical Engineering	10	*Ing. Químico*
Economics	10	*Economista*
Industrial Engineering	10	*Ing. Industrial*
Mechanical Engineering	10	*Ing. Mecáncio*
Petroleum Engineering	10	*Ing. de Petróleos*

Fundación Universidad de Bogotá "Jorge Tadeo Lozano"
Calle 23 No. 4-47, Apartado Aéreo 34185, Bogotá.
Tel: Conm. 2412287, 2434932, 2434934, 2834750/30. Established 1954.
Enrollment: 6631. (private)

Undergraduate Programs of Study	Length	Title Awarded
Accounting, Public	8-10	Contador Público
Advertising Technology*	6	Tgo. en Publicidad
Agricultural Administration Technology*	6	Tgo. en Administración Agropecuaria
Agrology	11	Agrólogo
Architectural, Decorative & Advertising Design Technology*	5	Tgo. en Decoración y Dibujo Arquitectónico
Architectural Drafting and Engineering Technology*	5	Tgo. en Delineante de Arquitectura e Ingeniería
Business Administration	8-10	Administrador de Empresas
Data Processing Technology*	6	Tgo. en Sistematización de Datos
Diplomatic & International Studies	8	Diplomado en Estudios Diplomáticos e Internacionales
Economics	8-10	Economista
Fine Arts	8	Diplomado en Bellas Artes
Food Engineering	10	Ing. de Alimentos
Geographical Engineering	11	Ing. Geógrafo
Graphic Design Technology*	5	Tgo. en Diseño Gráfico
Industrial Design	10	Diseñador Industrial
International Commerce	9	Diplomado en Comercio Internacional
Marine Biology	10	Biólogo Marino
Marketing Technology*	6	Tgo. en Mercadotecnia
Social Communication	8	Comunicador Social

Seccional (Branch Campus)

Fundación Universidad de Bogotá "Jorge Tadeo Lozano"-Cartagena
Carrera 4 No. 38-40, Apartado Aéreo 1310, Cartagena.
Tel: 42314, 42417.
Enrollment: 806.

Undergraduate Programs of Study	Length	Title Awarded
Architecture	10	Arquitecto
Foreign Trade Administration	10-12	Administrador de Comercio Exterior
Tourism Administration Technology*	6	Tgo. en Administración de Empresas Turísticas

Fundación Universidad de la Sabana
Calle 70 No. 11-79, Bogotá.
Tel: 2496846, 2494507, 2490385, 2496862, 2496830.
Enrollment: 1959. (private)

Undergraduate Programs of Study	Length	Degree or Title Awarded
Business Administration	8	*Administrador de Empresas*
Education:		
Educational Administration & Supervision	8	*Lic. en Administración y Supervisión Educativa*
Educational Psychology	8	*Lic. en Psicología Educativa*
Social Sciences	8	*Lic. en Ciencias Sociales*
Fine Arts Teaching Technology*	6	*Tgo. en Enseñanza de las Bellas Artes*
Plastic Arts Technology*	6	*Tgo. en Artes Plásticas*
Preschool Educational Technology*	4	*Tgo. en Educación Pre-escolar*
Social Communication	8	*Comunicador Social*

Fundación Universidad del Norte
Km. 5 Carretera a Pto. Colombia, Apartado Postal 0809, Barranquilla.
Tel: Conm. 57720, 46741. Established 1965.
Enrollment: 2898. (private)

Undergraduate Programs of Study	Length	Title Awarded
Business Administration	10	*Administrador de Empresas*
Civil Engineering	10	*Ing. Civil*
Electrical Engineering#	4	—
Industrial Engineering	10	*Ing. Industrial*
Mechanical Engineering	10	*Ing. Mecánico*
Medicine	12	*Médico*
Nursing Technology*	6	*Tgo. en Enfermería*
Pediatric Nursing	8	NA
Psychology	10	*Psicólogo*
Systems & Computation Engineering#	4	—

Fundación Universidad de Administración y Finanzas y Tecnologías (EAFIT)
Medellín.
See Fundación Universidad Escuela de Administración y Finanzas y Tecnologías (EAFIT), Medellín.

Fundación Universidad Incca de Colombia
Bogotá.
See Universidad INCCA de Colombia, Bogotá.

Fundación Universidad San Martín
Bogotá.
Enrollment: 200. (private)

Instituto Colombiano de Estudios Superiores de Incolda (ICESI)
Cali.
See Corporación Instituto Colombiano de Estudios Superiores
de Incolda (ICESI), Cali.

Instituto Colombo Venezolano (ICOLVEN)
Carrera 84 No. 33A-1, Apartado Aéreo 877, Medellín.
Tel: 432269, 433928.
Enrollment: 124. (private)

Undergraduate Program of Study	Length	Title Awarded
Education: Theology	8	*Diplomado en Teología*

Instituto de Ciencias de la Salud
Medellín.
See Fundación Instituto de Ciencias de la Salud (CES), Medellín.

Instituto de Educación Familiar y Social "Nina Reyes de Valenzuela"
Calle 72 No. 11-41, Bogotá.
Tel: 2494959, 2523226.
Enrollment: 184. (private)

Undergraduate Programs of Study	Length	Degree or Title Awarded
Education: Preschool Education	8	*Lic. en Educación Pre-escolar*
Family & Social Education	8	*Profesional en Educación Familiar y Social*

Instituto Mariano
Calle 18 No. 34-104, Pasto.
Tel: 3616. Established 1967.
Enrollment: 857. (private)

Undergraduate Programs of Study	Length	Degree or Title Awarded
Accounting, Public	10	*Contador Público*
Education:		
Commerce & Accounting	8	*Lic. en Comercio y Contaduría*
Home Economics	8	*Lic. en Ciencias Económico Familiares*
Modern Languages (Spanish-English)	8	*Lic. en Lenguas Modernas (Español-Inglés)*
Philosophy & Theology	8	*Lic. en Filosofía y Teología*
Social Sciences	8	*Lic. en Ciencias Sociales*
Nursing	8	*Enfermero*

Instituto Técnico Universitario de Cundinamarca (ITUC)
Apartado Aéreo 3033, Apartado Postal 101, Fusagasugá.
Tel: 2144. Established 1969.
Enrollment: 723. (public/state)

Undergraduate Programs of Study	Length	Degree or Title Awarded
Agricultural Technology*	6	Tgo. en Producción Agrícola
Animal Science Technology*	6	Tgo. en Producción Animal
Education:		
Educational Administration	9	Lic. en Administración Educativa
Mathematics & Physics	9	Lic. en Matemáticas y Física
Physical Education	8	Lic. en Educación Física
Financial Administration Technology*	6-7	Tgo. en Administración Financiera

Instituto Técnico Universitario de Cundinamarca (ITUC)
Carrera 15 Calle 16, Girardot.
Tel: 6205. Established 1972.
Enrollment: 290. (public/state)

Undergraduate Programs of Study	Length	Degree or Title Awarded
Education: Biology & Chemistry	9	Lic. en Biología y Química
Social Sciences	9	Lic. en Ciencias Sociales
Nursing Technology*	6	Tgo. en Enfermería

Instituto Técnico Universitario de Cundinamarca (ITUC)
Calle 6 No. 9-80, Ubaté.
Tel: 3055, 3056. Established 1971.
Enrollment: 297. (public/state)

Undergraduate Programs of Study	Length	Degree or Title Awarded
Education:		
Mathematics & Physics	9	Lic. en Matemáticas y Física
Modern Languages (Spanish-English)	9	Lic. en Lenguas Modernas (Español-Inglés)
Financial Administration Technology*	7	Tgo. en Administración Financiera

Instituto Universitario de Economía Social y Cooperativismo (INDESCO)
Avenida Caracas No. 37-63, Apartado Aéreo 13673, Bogotá.
Tel: 2453217, 2455216, 2328474. Established 1958.
Enrollment: 1364. (private)

Undergraduate Programs of Study	Length	Degree or Title Awarded
Business Administration	10	Administrador de Empresas
Economics	10	Economista

Education: Educational	8	*Lic. en Administración Educativa*
Administration		
Sociology	8	*Sociólogo*

Seccionales (Branch Campuses)

Instituto Universitario de Economía Social y Cooperativismo (INDESCO)
Calle 9A No. 12-09 Barrio Colombia, Barrancabermeja.
Tel: 4120.
Enrollment: 409.

Undergraduate Programs of Study	Length	Title Awarded
Business Administration	10	*Administrador de Empresas*
Economics	10	*Economista*

Instituto Universitario de Economía Social y Cooperativismo (INDESCO)
Carrera 33 Calle 30, Bucaramanga.
Tel: 55404, 54229.
Enrollment: 2096.

Undergraduate Programs of Study	Length	Degree or Title Awarded
Business Administration	10	*Administrador de Empresas*
Economics	10	*Economista*
Education: Educational	8	*Lic. en Administración Educativa*
Administration		
Sociology	10	*Sociólogo*

Instituto Universitario de Economía Social y Cooperativismo (INDESCO)
Carrera 42 No. 49-59, Medellín.
Tel: 399625, 398371.
Enrollment: 2198.

Undergraduate Programs of Study	Length	Degree or Title Awarded
Business Administration	10	*Administrador de Empresas*
Economics	10	*Economista*
Education: Educational	8	*Lic. en Administración Educativa*
Administration		

Pontificia Universidad Javeriana
Carrera 7a. No. 40-62, Bogotá.
Tel: 2322040, 2455021. Established 1623.
Enrollment: 8907. (private)

Undergraduate Programs of Study	Length	Degree or Title Awarded
Accounting, Public	10	*Contador Público*
Architecture	10	*Arquitecto*
Bacteriology	8	*Bacteriólogo*
Biology	8	*Biólogo*

Business Administration	10	*Administrador de Empresas*
Civil Engineering	10	*Ing. Civil*
Dentistry	10	*Odontólogo*
Economics	10	*Economista*
Education: Biology	8	*Lic. en Biología*
Chemistry	8	*Lic. en Química*
Mathematics	8	*Lic. en Matemáticas*
Modern Languages	8	*Lic. en Lenguas Modernas*
Philology & Literature	8	*Lic. en Filología y Literatura*
Philosphy	8	*Lic. en Filosofía*
Philosophy & Letters	8	*Lic. en Filosofía y Letras*
Physics	8	*Lic. en Física*
Physics & Mathematics	8	*Lic. en Física y Matemáticas*
Social Sciences	8	*Lic. en Ciencias Sociales*
Spanish Philology	8	*Lic. en Filología Española*
Theology	8	*Lic. en Teología*
Electronic Engineering	10	*Ing. Electrónico*
Industrial Design	10	*Diseñador Industrial*
Industrial Engineering	10	*Ing. Industrial*
Law	10	*Abogado*
Library Science	8	*Bibliotecólogo*
Mathematics	8	*Matemático*
Medicine	12	*Médico*
Nursing	8	*Enfermero*
Nutrition & Dietetics	8	*Nutricionista y Dietista*
Philosophy	8	*Filósofo*
Philosophy & Letters	8	*Diplomado en Filosofía y Letras*
Psychology	10	*Psicólogo*
Religious Studies	8	*Profesional en Estudios Religiosos*
Social Communication	8	*Comunicador Social*
Theology	8	*Teólogo*

**Specialist Programs of Study. Title Awarded—*Especialista en . . . Administración de Salud; Anestesiología; Cirugía General; Derecho Comercial; Derecho de Familia; Derecho Laboral; Endodoncia; Estomatología; Gineco-Obstetricia; Medicina Interna; Neumología; Neurocirugía; Neurología; Oftalmología; Ortodoncia; Ortopedia y Traumatología; Otorrinolaringología; Patología; Pediatría; Periodoncia; Psiquiatría; Radiología; Radioterapia.*

**Master's Programs of Study. Title Awarded—*Magister en . . . Administración de Salud; Alimentación y Nutrición; Biología; Centrales Hidroeléctricas; Derecho Comercial-Seguros; Derecho Comercial-Sociedades; Desarrollo Rural; Economía; Educación Comparada; Estudios Políticos; Filosofía y Letras (Filosofía, Historia, Literatura); Investigación y Tecnología Educativas; Microbiología; Población; Restauración de Monumentos Arquitectónicos; Planeación Urbana y Regional; Teología.*

**Doctoral Programs of Study. Title Awarded—*Doctor en . . . Derecho Canónico; Filosofía; Filosofía y Letras (Filosofía, Historia, Literatura); Estudios Políticos; Teología.*

**Sources for these programs include ICFES (1983), and the Pontificia Universidad Javeriana (1983).

Seccional (Branch Campus)

Pontificia Universidad Javeriana-Cali
Carrera 29 No. 6-60, Apartado Aéreo 8264, Cali.
Tel: 682030. Enrollment: 1138.

Undergraduate Programs of Study	Length	Title Awarded
Accounting, Public	10	*Contador Público*
Industrial Engineering	10	*Ing. Industrial*

Unidad Central del Valle del Cauca
Carrera 26 No. 30-58, Tuluá.
Tel: 4375, 4337, 2202. Established 1971.
Enrollment: 1092. (public/municipal)

Undergraduate Programs of Study	Length	Degree or Title Awarded
Accounting, Public	10	*Contador Público*
Business Administration	10	*Administrador de Empresas*
Education: Physical Education	10	*Lic. en Educación Física*
Social Sciences	9	*Lic. en Ciencias Sociales*
Law	12	*Abogado*

Universidad Autónoma del Caribe
Carrera 46 No. 88-26, Apartado Aéreo 50826, Barranquilla.
Tel: 350826, 355804. Established 1967.
Enrollment: 6104. (private)

Undergraduate Programs of Study	Length	Title Awarded
Accounting, Public	10	*Contador Público*
Architecture	10	*Arquitecto*
Business Administration	10	*Administrador de Empresas*
Hotel & Tourism Administration	10	*Administrador Hotelería y Turismo*
Social Communication	8	*Comunicador Social*
Sociology	10	*Sociólogo*
Textile Design Technology*	6	*Tgo. en Diseño Textil*

Universidad Autónoma Latinoamericana
Carrera 55 No. 49-51, Apartado Aéreo 3455, Medellín.
Tel: 313224 a 36, 423239. Established 1966.
Enrollment: 2419. (private)

Undergraduate Programs of Study	Length	Degree or Title Awarded
Accounting, Public	10	*Contador Público*
Economics	10	*Economista*
Education: History & Philosophy	8	*Lic. en Historia y Filosofía*
Philosophy & History	8	*Lic. en Filosofía e Historia*
Industrial Engineering	10	*Ing. Industrial*

Law	10	*Abogado*
Sociology	8	*Sociólogo*

Universidad Católica de Manizales
Carrera 23 No. 60-63, Zona 4, Apartado Aéreo 357, Manizales.
Tel: 51412, 53121, 55470. Established 1954.
Enrollment: 1152. (private)

Undergraduate Programs of Study	Length	Degree or Title Awarded
Architectural Drafting Technology*	6	*Tgo. en Delineante de Arquitectura*
Bacteriology & Clinical Laboratory	8	*Bacteriólogo y Laboratorista Clínico*
Education:		
Educational Administration	8	*Lic. en Administración Educativa*
Orientation & Counseling	8	*Lic. en Orientación y Consejería*
Religious Studies	8	*Lic. en Ciencias Religiosas*
Phonoaudiology	8	*Fonoaudiólogo*

Universidad Católica Popular del Risaralda
Calle 20 No. 3-65, Apartado Aéreo 2435, Pereira.
Tel: 46524. Established 1976.
Enrollment: 547. (private)

Undergraduate Programs of Study	Length	Title Awarded
Business Administration	10-11	*Administrador de Empresas*
Industrial Economics	11	*Economista Industrial*

Universidad de Antioquia
Ciudad Universitaria, Apartado Aéreo 1226, Medellín.
Tel: 330599, 334141. Established 1801.
Enrollment: 15,732. (public/state)

Undergraduate Programs of Study	Length	Degree or Title Awarded
Accounting, Public	10	*Contador Público*
Animal Science	10	*Zootecnista*
Anthropology	8	*Antropólogo*
Bacteriology & Clinical Laboratory	8	*Bacteriólogo y Laboratorista Clínico*
Biology	8	*Biólogo*
Business Administration	10	*Administrador de Empresas*
Chemical Engineering	10	*Ing. Químico*
Chemistry	8	*Químico*
Communication Sciences	8	*Comunicador Social*
Dentistry	10	*Odontólogo*
Economics	10	*Economista*
Education:		
Agriculture & Animal Science	8	*Lic. en Agropecuarias*
Biblical Studies	8	*Lic. en Estudios Bíblicos*
Biology-Chemistry	8	*Lic. en Biología y Química*

Business Teaching	8	*Lic. en Docencia Comercial*
Electrotechnics	8	*Lic. en Electrotecnia*
English-Spanish	8	*Lic. en Inglés-Castellano*
French Literature	8	*Lic. en Francés-Literatura*
History & Geography	8	*Lic. en Historia y Geografía*
History-Philosophy	8	*Lic. en Historia-Filosofía*
Industrial Mechanics	8	*Lic. en Mecánica Industrial*
Mathematics-Physics	8	*Lic. en Matemáticas-Física*
Musical Education	8	*Lic. en Educación Musical*
Physical Education	8	*Lic. en Educación Física*
Plastic Arts	8	*Lic. en Artes Plásticas*
School Administration	8	*Lic. en Administración Escolar*
Spanish Language-Literature	8	*Lic. en Castellano-Literatura*
Electrical Engineering	10	*Ing. Eléctrico*
Electronic Engineering	10	*Ing. Electrónico*
English	8	*Diplomado en Inglés*
Food Technology*	6	*Tgo. de Alimentos*
History	10	*Historiador*
Industrial Engineering	10	*Ing. Industrial*
Law & Political Science	10	*Abogado*
Library Science	8	*Bibliotecólogo*
Mathematics	8	*Matemático*
Mechanical Engineering	10	*Ing. Mecánico*
Medicine	14	*Médico*
Metallurgical Engineering	10	*Ing. Metalúrgico*
Nursing	8	*Enfermero*
Nutrition & Dietetics	8	*Nutricionista y Dietista*
Pharmacy	10	*Químico Farmaceuta*
Pharmaceutical Technology*	6	*Regente en Farmacia*
Philosophy & Letters	10	*Profesional en Filosofía y Letras*
Physics	8	*Físico*
Plastic Arts	8	*Maestro en Artes Plásticas*
Sanitary Engineering	10	*Ing. Sanitario*
Social Work	8	*Trabajador Social*
Sociology	8	*Sociólogo*
Veterinary Medicine	10	*Médico Veterinario*

Specialist Programs of Study. Title Awarded—*Especialista en . . . Administración de Atención Médica y Hospitalaria; Anatomía Patológica; Anestesia y Reanimación; Cirugía General; Cirugía Infantil; Cirugía Plástica; Dermatología; Endoscopia Digestiva; Epidemiología; Medicina Física y Rehabilitación; Medicina Interna; Nefrología; Neurocirugía; Obstetricia y Ginecología; Oftalmología; Ortopedia y Traumatología; Otorrinolaringología; Pediatría; Planificación de la Salud; Política Económica; Psiquiatría; Radiología; Radioterapia; Urología.*

Master's Programs of Study. Title Awarded—*Magister en . . . Administración Educativa; Bioquímica; Docencia y Tecnología Educativa; Farmacología; Física; Fisiología; Investigación Socio-Educativa; Investigación Psicopedagógica; Microbiología Médica; Morfología; Orientación y Consejería; Parasitología; Salud Pública.*

Universidad de Caldas
Calle 65 No. 26-10, Apartado Aéreo 275, Manizales.
Tel: 51712, 54961, Conm. 55240. Established 1943.
Enrollment: 3743. (public/national)

Undergraduate Programs of Study	Length	Degree or Title Awarded
Agronomy	10	*Agrónomo*
Education: Biology & Chemistry	8	*Lic. en Biología y Química*
Chemistry & Biology	8	*Lic. en Química y Biología*
History & Geography	8	*Lic. en Historia y Geografía*
Modern Languages	8	*Lic. en Lenguas Modernas*
Home Economics	8	*Economista del Hogar*
Law	10	*Abogado*
Medicine	12	*Médico*
Musical Education	8	*Maestro en Educación Musical*
Nursing	8	*Enfermero*
Philosophy & Letters	8	*Diplomado en Filosofía y Letras*
Plastic Arts	8	*Maestro en Artes Plásticas*
Social Work	8	*Trabajador Social*
Veterinary Medicine	10	*Médico Veterinario*

Specialist Programs of Study. Title Awarded—*Especialista en . . . Anatomía Patológica; Anestesiología; Cirugía General; Cirugía Pediátrica; Cirugía Plástica; Dermatología; Gastroenterología; Ginecología y Obstetricia; Medicina Interna; Oftalmología; Otorrinolaringología; Pediatría; Psiquiatría.*

Master's Programs of Study. Title Awarded—*Maestría en . . . Derecho Administrativo; Filosofía y Ciencias Jurídicas.*

Universidad de Cartagena
Carrera 6 No. 36-100 Calle de la Universidad, Apartado Aéreo 2086, Cartagena.
Tel: 47121, 40185. Established 1774.
Enrollment: 4223. (public/state)

Undergraduate Programs of Study	Length	Title Awarded
Accounting, Public	10	*Contador Público*
Business Administration	10	*Administrador de Empresas*
Chemistry & Pharmacy	10	*Químico Farmaceuta*
Civil Engineering	10	*Ing. Civil*
Dentistry	10	*Odontólogo*
Economics	9	*Economista*
Law	10	*Abogado*
Medicine	14	*Médico Cirujano*
Nursing	8	*Enfermero*
Social Work	8	*Trabajador Social*

Specialist Programs of Study. Title Awarded—*Especialista en . . . Administración de Empresas; Anestesiología; Cirugía General; Gineco-Obstetricia; Medicina Interna; Neurocirugía; Oftalmología; Ortopedia; Otorrinolaringología; Patología Oral (Estomatología); Pediatría; Radiología; Urología.*

Universidad de Córdoba
Carretera a Cereté Km. 5, Apartado Aéreo 354, Montería.
Tel: 8499, 4600, 3278, Conm. 3381. Established 1962.
Enrollment: 2893. (public/national)

Undergraduate Programs of Study	Length	Degree or Title Awarded
Agronomy	10	*Agrónomo*
Education: Biology & Chemistry	10	*Lic. en Biología y Química*
Chemistry & Biology	10	*Lic. en Química y Biología*
Mathematics & Physics	10	*Lic. en Matemáticas y Física*
Social Sciences	10	*Lic. en Ciencias Sociales*
Nursing Technology*	6	*Tgo. en Enfermería*
Veterinary Medicine & Animal Science	10	*Médico Veterinario y Zootecnista*

Universidad del Atlántico
Carrera 43 No. 50-53, Apartado Aéreo 1890, Barranquilla.
Tel: 313513, 315633. Established 1941.
Enrollment: 8798. (public/state)

Undergraduate Programs of Study	Length	Degree or Title Awarded
Accounting, Public	10	*Contador Público*
Architecture	10	*Arquitecto*
Business Administration	10	*Administrador de Empresas*
Chemical Engineering	10	*Ing. Químico*
Chemistry & Pharmacy	10	*Químico y Farmacéutico*
Economics	10	*Economista*
Education:		
Biology & Chemistry	8	*Lic. en Biología y Química*
Languages	8	*Lic. en Idiomas*
Mathematics	8	*Lic. en Matemáticas*
Musical Education	8	*Lic. en Educación Musical*
Social & Economic Sciences	8	*Lic. en Ciencias Sociales*
Law	10	*Abogado*
Nutrition & Dietetics	8	*Nutricionista y Dietista*
Painting	10	*Maestro en Pintura*

Universidad del Cauca
Calle 5 No. 4-70, Popayán.
Tel: 1893, 3020, 4115. Established 1964.
Enrollment: 2859. (public/national)

Undergraduate Programs of Study	Length	Degree or Title Awarded
Accounting, Public	10	*Contador Público*
Anthropology	8	*Antropólogo*
Civil Engineering	10	*Ing. Civil*
Education:		
Biology	10	*Lic. en Biología*

Mathematics	10	Lic. en Matemáticas
Modern Languages (Spanish & English)	10	Lic. en Lenguas Modernas (Español y Inglés)
Modern Languages (Spanish & French)	10	Lic. en Lenguas Modernas (Español e Francés)
Social Sciences (Geography)	10	Lic. en Ciencias Sociales (Geografía)
Social Sciences (History)	10	Lic. en Ciencias Sociales (Historia)
Electronic Engineering & Telecommunications	10	Ing. Electricidad y Telecomunicaciones
Geotechnology*	6	Geotecnólogo
Law	8	Abogado
Medicine	14	Médico
Music	8	Maestro en Música
Nursing Technology*	6	Tgo. en Enfermería
Philosophy	8	Filósofo
Plastic Arts	8	Maestro en Artes Plásticas
Spanish Language & Literature	8	Profesor en Literatura y Lengua Española

Specialist Programs of Study. Title Awarded—*Especialista en . . . Cirugía; Gineco-Obstetricia y Patología; Hematología; Ingeniería Civil-Vías; Medicina Interna; Patología; Pediatría.*

Master's Programs of Study. Title Awarded—*Magister en . . . Electrónica y Telecomunicaciones; Ingeniería Civil-Vías; Telemática.*

Universidad de los Andes
Carrera 1 Este No. 18A-10, Apartado Aéreo 4976, Bogotá.
Tel: 2437474. Established 1949.
Enrollment: 4212. (private)

Undergraduate Programs of Study	Length	Title Awarded
Anthropology	8	Antropólogo
Architecture	10	Arquitecto
Bacteriology	8	Bacteriólogo
Biology	8	Biólogo
Business Administration	10	Administrador de Empresas
Civil Engineering	10	Ing. Civil
Economics	10	Economista
Electrical Engineering	10	Ing. Eléctrico
Industrial Engineering	10	Ing. Industrial
Law	10	Abogado
Mathematics	8	Matemático
Mechanical Engineering	10	Ing. Mecánico
Microbiology	8	Microbiólogo
Modern Languages	8	Profesional en Lenguas Modernas
Philosophy & Letters	8	Diplomado en Filosofía y Letras
Physics	9	Físico
Political Science	8	Diplomado en Ciencias Políticas
Psychology	10	Psicólogo

Systems & Computation   10   *Ing. Sistemas y Computación*
Engineering

Specialist Programs of Study. Title Awarded—*Especialista en . . . Derecho Comercial y Empresas Transnacionales; Derecho de Familia; Derecho Público y Económico; Planificación y Administración del Desarrollo Regional.*

Master's Programs of Study. Title Awarded—*Magister en . . . Administración; Biología; Ciencia Política; Economía; Ingeniería Civil; Ingeniería de Sistemas y Computación; Ingeniería Eléctrica; Ingeniería Industrial; Ingeniería Mecánica; Lingüística Aplicada; Matemáticas; Microbiología; Planeación y Administración del Desarrollo Regional.*

Universidad del Quindío
Carrera 15 Calle 12, Apartado Aéreo 460, Armenia.
Tel: 49341, 41501. Established 1961.
Enrollment: 4828. (public/state)

Undergraduate Programs of Study	Length	Degree or Title Awarded
Accounting, Public	10	*Contador Público*
Civil Engineering	10	*Ing. Civil*
Education:		
Biology & Chemistry	8	*Lic. en Biología y Química*
Educational Psychology	8	*Lic. en Psicopedagogía*
Educational Technology	8	*Lic. en Tecnología Educativa*
Linguistics & Literature	8	*Lic. en Lingüística y Literatura*
Mathematics	8	*Lic. en Matemáticas*
Modern Languages	8	*Lic. en Lenguas Modernas*
Physics	8	*Lic. en Física*
Social Sciences	9	*Lic. en Ciencias Sociales*
Electrical Engineering[#]	4	—
Industrial Engineering[#]	4	—
Mechanical Engineering[#]	4	—
Medicine	NA	NA
Topographical Technology*	6	*Tgo. en Topografía*

Universidad del Tolima
Santa Helena, Apartado Aéreo 546, Ibagué.
Tel: 32544, 34219, 34224, 32733. Established 1945.
Enrollment: 4082. (public/state)

Undergraduate Programs of Study	Length	Degree or Title Awarded
Agronomy Engineering	10	*Ing. Agrónomo*
Architectural Drafting Technology*	6	*Tgo. en Dibujo Arquitectónico y de Ingeniería*
Business Administration	10	*Administrador de Empresas*
Education:		
Biology & Chemistry	8	*Lic. en Biología y Química*
Mathematics & Physics	8	*Lic. en Matemáticas y Física*

Social Sciences (History & Geography)	8	Lic. en Ciencias Sociales
Spanish-English	8	Lic. en Español-Inglés
Electrical Engineering#	4	—
Forestry Engineering	10	Ing. Forestal
Industrial Engineering#	4	—
Mechanical Engineering#	4	—
Topographical Technology*	6	Tgo. en Topografía
Veterinary Medicine & Animal Sciences	10	Médico Veterinario y Zootecnista

Universidad del Valle
Barrio San Bernardo, Apartado Aéreo 2188, Cali.
Tel: 392207, 392310, 391486. Established 1945.
Enrollment: 7061. (public/state)

Undergraduate Programs of Study	Length	Degree or Title Awarded
Accounting, Public	10	Contador Público
Agricultural Engineering	10	Ing. Agrícola
Architecture	12	Arquitecto
Biology	8	Biólogo
Business Administration	11	Administrador de Empresas
Business Administration Technology*	6	Tgo. en Administrador de Empresas
Chemical Engineering	10	Ing. Químico
Chemistry	8	Químico
Chemistry Technology*	6	Tgo. en Química
Civil Engineering	10	Ing. Civil
Dentistry	8	Odontólogo
Education:		
Animal Sciences	8	Lic. en Ciencias Agropecuarias (located in Buga)
Biology-Chemistry	8-10	Lic. en Biología-Química
Electricity & Electronics	8	NA
Literature	8	Lic. en Literatura
Mathematics	8	Lic. en Matemáticas
Mathematics-Physics	8-10	Lic. en Matemáticas-Física
Modern Languages	8	Lic. en Lenguas Modernas
Philosophy	8-10	Lic. en Filosofía
Physical Education & Health	8	Lic. en Educación Física y Salud
Electrical Engineering	10	Ing. Electricista
General Economics	8	Economista
History	8	Historiador
Industrial Engineering	10	Ing. Industrial
Letters	8	Diplomado en Letras
Mathematics	8	Matemático
Medical Laboratory Technology*	6	Tgo. en Laboratorio Médico
Medicine	14	Médico Cirujano
Musical Education	8	Maestro en Educación Musical
Nursing	8	Enfermero
Nursing (by distance)‖	5	NA

Nursing Technology*	6	Tgo. en Enfermería
Philosophy	8	Filósofo
Physics	8	Físico
Physiotherapy	8	Fisioterapeuta
Psychology	8	Psicólogo
Sanitary Engineering	12	Ing. Sanitario
Social Communication	8	Comunicador Social
Social Work	8	Trabajador Social
Sociology	10	Sociólogo
Statistics	10	NA
Topography Technology*	6	NA

Specialist Programs of Study. Title Awarded—*Especialista en . . . Anestesiología; Cirugía General; Dermatología; Ginecología y Obstetricia; Medicina Física y Rehabilitación; Medicina Interna; Neurocirugía; Oftalmología; Ortopedia y Traumatología; Otorrinolaringología; Patología; Patología y Laboratorio Clínico; Pediatría; Psiquiatría; Radiodiagnóstico; Radioterapia; Urología.*

Master's Programs of Study. Title Awarded—*Magister en . . . Administración de Salud; Administración Educacional; Administración Industrial; Bioquímica; Ciencias-Física; Ciencias–Matemáticas; Ciencias–Química; Enfermería Clínica; Enfermería Psiquiátrica y Salud Mental; Farmacología; Fisiología; Ingeniería Industrial y de Sistemas; Lingüística y Español; Microbiología; Morfología; Salud Pública.*

Universidad de Medellín
Carrera 87 No. 30-65 Los Alpes Belén, Apartado Aéreo 1983, Medellín.
Tel: 383886, 381252, 383906, 316586. Established 1954.
Enrollment: 5102. (private)

Undergraduate Programs of Study	Length	Degree or Title Awarded
Accounting, Public	11	Contador Público
Administrative Sciences	10	Profesional en Ciencias Administrativas
Civil Engineering	10	Ing. Civil
Education:		
Educational Administration	8	Lic. en Administración Educativa
Mathematics	8	Lic. en Matemáticas
Spanish Literature	8	Lic. en Español-Literatura
Industrial Economics	10	Economista Industrial
Law	10	Abogado
Statistics	10	Estadístico

Universidad de Nariño
Carrera 25 No. 18-109, Apartado Aéreo 505-626, Pasto.
Tel: 5652, 5654, 4937, 1652, 1653. Established 1967.
Enrollment: 3992. (public/state)

Undergraduate Programs of Study	Length	Degree or Title Awarded
Agronomy Engineering	10	Ing. Agrónomo

Animal Sciences	10	*Zootecnista*
Civil Engineering	10	*Ing. Civil*
Economics	10-12	*Economista*
Education:		
Chemistry & Biology	8	*Lic. en Química y Biología*
Modern Languages	10	*Lic. en Lenguas Modernas*
Philosophy & Letters	8-10	*Lic. en Filosofía y Letras*
Physics & Mathematics	8-10	*Lic. en Física y Matemáticas*
Plastic Arts	8-10	*Lic. en Artes Plásticas*
Social Sciences	10	*Lic. en Ciencias Sociales*
Law	10	*Abogado*
Plastic Arts	8-10	*Maestro en Artes Plásticas*

Universidad de Pamplona
Carrera 4 No. 4-38, Pamplona.
Tel: 2960, 9701. Established 1960.
Enrollment: 2089. (public/state)

Undergraduate Programs of Study	Length	Degree Awarded
Education:		
Biology & Chemistry	8	*Lic. en Biología y Química*
Chemistry & Biology	8	*Lic. en Química y Biología*
Educational Administration & Planning	8	*Lic. en Administración y Planeamiento Educativo*
Educational Psychology	8	*Lic. en Psicopedagogía*
English-French	8	*Lic. en Inglés-Francés*
Linguistics & Literature	8	*Lic. en Lingüística y Literatura*
Mathematics & Physics	8	*Lic. en Matemáticas y Física*
Orientation & Counseling	8	*Lic. en Orientación y Consejería*
Physical Education	8	*Lic. en Educación Física*
Physics & Mathematics	8	*Lic. en Física y Matemáticas*
Social Sciences (History-Geography, Geography-History)	8	*Lic. en Ciencias Sociales*

Universidad de San Buenaventura
Calle 73 No. 10-45, Apartado Aéreo 53746, Bogotá.
Tel: 2354942, 2352922. Established 1715.
Enrollment: 1531. (private)

Undergraduate Programs of Study	Length	Degree or Title Awarded
Education:		
Educational Administration	8	*Lic. en Administración Educativa*
Preschool Education	8	*Lic. en Educación Pre-escolar*
Primary Education	9	*Lic. en Educación Primaria*
Philosophy	8	*Filósofo*
Theology	8	*Teólogo*

Seccionales (Branch Campuses)

Universidad de San Buenaventura-Cali
Carrera 5a. No. 9-02, Cali.
Tel: 781511, 892594.
Enrollment: 1873.

Undergraduate Programs of Study	Length	Degree or Title Awarded
Accounting, Public	10	*Contador Público*
Economics	10	*Economista*
Education:		
History-Philosophy	10	*Lic. en Historia y Filosofía*
Mathematics-Physics	10	*Lic. en Matemáticas-Física*
Preschool Education	10	*Lic. en Educación Pre-escolar*
Primary Education	10	*Lic. en Educación Primaria*
Religious Studies	9	*Lic. en Ciencias Religiosas*
Spanish-Literature	10	*Lic. en Español y Literatura*
Law	10	*Abogado*

Universidad de San Buenaventura-Medellín
Medellín.
Tel: 411856, 427024.
Enrollment: 1300.

Undergraduate Programs of Study	Length	Degree or Title Awarded
Education:		
Agricultural Technology§	3	*Lic. en Tecnología Agropecuaria*
Cost & Auditing Technology§	3	*Lic. en Tecnología de Costos y Auditoría*
Data Systems§	3	*Lic. en Sistematización de Datos*
Educational Administration	8	*Lic. en Administración Educativa*
Electronics Technology§	3	*Lic. en Tecnología Electrónica*
Industrial Processes§	3	*Lic. en Procesos Industriales*
Industrial Supervision§	3	*Lic. en Supervisión Industrial*
Industrial Technology§	3	*Lic. en Tecnología Industrial*
Mechanical Technology§	3	*Lic. en Tecnología Mecánica*
Preschool Education	8	*Lic. en Educación Pre-escolar*
Psychology	10	*Psicólogo*
Sociology	10	*Sociólogo*

Universidad de Santo Tomás
Carrera 9 No. 51-23, Bogotá.
Tel: 2480482, 2483641, Conm. 2357192, 2357312. Established 1580.
Enrollment: 6019. (private)

Undergraduate Programs of Study	Length	Degree or Title Awarded
Accounting, Public	10	*Contador Público*
Civil Engineering	10	*Ing. Civil*
Economics	10	*Economista*

Education: Philosophy & Letters	8	*Lic. en Filosofía y Letras*
Law	10	*Abogado*
Philosophy & Religion	8	*Profesor en Filosofía y Ciencias Religiosas*
Psychology	10	*Psicólogo*
Sociology	10	*Sociólogo*

Specialist Programs of Study. Title Awarded—*Especialista en . . . Derecho de Familia; Derecho de Integración.*

Master's Programs of Study. Title Awarded—*Magister en . . . Administración Comercial; Administración de la Construcción; Administración de Sistemas; Administración Educativa; Administración Financiera; Administración y Planeación Social; Auditoría de Sistemas de Computación; Diseño y Evaluación de Proyectos de Desarrollo Socioeconómico; Filosofía Latinoamericana; Investigación y Docencia Universitaria; Planeación y Desarrollo; Psicología Clínica; Psicología Familiar.*

Seccional (Branch Campus)

Universidad de Santo Tomás-Bucaramanga
Carrera 19 No. 9-50, Bucaramanga.
Tel: 32342, 31383, 32343, 32351, 32853.
Enrollment: 2548.

Undergraduate Programs of Study	Length	Title Awarded
Accounting, Public	10	*Contador Público*
Architecture	10	*Arquitecto*
Economics	10	*Economista*
Law	10	*Abogado*

Master's Programs of Study. Title Awarded—*Magister en . . . Administración Educativa; Control Financiero; Investigación y Docencia Universitaria; Relaciones Industriales.*

Universidad de Sucre
Calle 19 No. 22-58, Apartado Aéreo 406, Sincelejo.
Enrollment: 344. (public/state)

Undergraduate Programs of Study	Length	Degree or Title Awarded
Agricultural Engineering	10	*Ing. Agrícola*
Agricultural Production Technology*	6	*Tgo. en Producción Agropecuaria*
Education: Mathematics	8	*Lic. en Matemáticas*

Universidad Distrital "Francisco José de Caldas"
Carrera 8a. No. 40-78, Apartado Aéreo 8668, Bogotá.
Tel: 2457088, 2450440. Established 1948.
Enrollment: 3239. (public/municipal)

Undergraduate Programs of Study	Length	Degree or Title Awarded
Cadastral & Geodesic Engineering	10	*Ing. Catastral y Geodesta*
Education: Biology	8	*Lic. en Biología*
Chemistry	8	*Lic. en Química*
Mathematics	8	*Lic. en Matemáticas*
Physics	8	*Lic. en Física*
Social Sciences	8	*Lic. en Ciencias Sociales*
Electronic Engineering	10	*Ing. Electrónico*
Forestry Engineering	10	*Ing. Forestal*
Industrial Engineering	10	*Ing. Industrial*
Systems Engineering	10	*Ing. de Sistemas*
Topography Technology*	6	*Tgo. en Topografía*

Universidad Escuela Superior de Administración y Finanzas y Tecnologías
Medellín.
See Fundación Universidad Escuela de Administración y Finanzas y Tecnologías (EAFIT), Medellín.

Universidad Experimental de la Guajira
Calle 26 Carrera 6, Apartado Aéreo 172, Riohacha.
Enrollment: 332. (public/state)

Undergraduate Programs of Study	Length	Title Awarded
Business Administration	10	*Administrador de Empresas*

Universidad Externado de Colombia
Calle 12 No. 1-17 Este, Apartado Aéreo 034141, Bogotá.
Tel: 2826066, 2839261, 2415038. Established 1886.
Enrollment: 6833. (private)

Undergraduate Programs of Study	Length	Degree or Title Awarded
Accounting, Public	10	*Contador Público*
Business Administration	10	*Administrador de Empresas*
Economics	10	*Economista*
Education: Education & Psychology	9	*Lic. en Pedagogía y Psicología*
Social Sciences	9	*Lic. en Ciencias Sociales*
Law	10	*Abogado*
Social Communication	8	*Comunicador Social*
Social Work	8	*Trabajador Social*
Tourism & Hotel Management	10	*Gerente Hotelero y de Turismo*

Specialist Programs of Study. Title Awarded—*Especialista en . . . Ciencias Penales; Criminología; Derecho Administrativo; Derecho Comercial; Derecho de Familia; Derecho Laboral.*

Master's Programs of Study. Title Awarded—*Magister en . . . Administración y Supervisión Educativa; Finanzas-Sistemas y Ciencias Contables; Orientación y Asesoría Educativa; Política Social.*

Universidad Francisco de Paula Santander
Avenida Gran Colombia No. 12E-96, Cúcuta.
Tel: 21371, 40072, 44253. Established 1962.
Enrollment: 3265. (public/state)

Undergraduate Programs of Study	Length	Degree or Title Awarded
Accounting, Public	10	*Contador Público*
Agronomy	10	*Ing. Agrónomo*
Architectural Drafting &	6	*Tgo. Delineante de Arquitectura e*
Engineering Technology*		*Ingeniería*
Business Administration	10	*Administrador de Empresas*
Chemical Engineering#	4	—
Chemical Technology*	6	NA
Civil Engineering	10	*Ing. Civil*
Civil Works Technology*	6	*Tgo. en Obras Civiles*
Economics#	4	—
Education:		
Animal Science‡§	3	NA
Architectural Drafting &	3	*Lic. Delineante de Arquitectura e*
Engineering‡§		*Ingeniería*
Biology & Chemistry	10	*Lic. en Biología y Química*
Civil Works†§	3	*Lic. en Obras Civiles*
Electromechanics†§	3	*Lic. en Electromecánica*
Engineering Laboratory†§	3	*Lic. en Laboratorio de Ingeniería*
Mathematics & Physics	10	*Lic. en Matemáticas y Física*
Electrical Engineering#	4	NA
Electromechanical Technology*	6	*Tgo. en Electromecánica*
Mechanical Engineering	10	*Ing. Mecánico*
Mining Technology*	6	NA
Nursing Technology*	6	*Tgo. en Enfermería*

Seccionales (Branch Campuses)

Universidad Francisco de Paula Santander-Bochalema
Bochalema (N. de S.).
Established 1962.
Enrollment: 101.

Undergraduate Programs of Study	Length	Title Awarded
Animal Science Technology*	6	*Tgo. Agropecuario*

Universidad Francisco de Paula Santander-Ocaña
Ocaña.
Tel: 3344, 2222, 2271.
Enrollment: 236.

Undergraduate Programs of Study	Length	Degree or Title Awarded
Agricultural Production Technology*	6	*Tgo. en Producción Agropecuaria*
Education: Mathematics & Physics	8	*Lic. en Matemáticas y Física*

Universidad INCCA de Colombia
Carrera 13 No. 24-15, Apartado Aéreo 14817, Bogotá.
Tel: 2347078, 2347552. Established 1955.
Enrollment: 7607. (private)

Undergraduate Programs of Study	Length	Degree or Title Awarded
Agricultural Economics	11	*Economista Agrario*
Business Economics	12	*Economista de Empresas*
Education:		
Biology & Chemistry	9	*Lic. en Biología y Química*
Educational Administration	9	*Lic. en Administración Educativa*
Instructional Communication & Technology	9	NA
Mathematics & Physics	9	*Lic. en Matemáticas y Física*
Philology & Languages	9	*Lic. en Filología e Idiomas*
Preschool Education	9	*Lic. en Educación Pre-escolar*
Food Engineering	11	*Ing. de Alimentos*
Industrial Engineering	11	*Ing. Industrial*
Law	10	*Abogado*
Mechanical Engineering	12	*Ing. Mecánico*
Psychology	10	*Psicólogo*
Systems Engineering	12	*Ing. de Sistemas*

Universidad Industrial de Santander
Ciudad Universitaria, Apartado Aéreo 678, Bucaramanga.
Tel: Conm. 56141-49. Established 1947.
Enrollment: 4831. (public/state)

Undergraduate Programs of Study	Length	Degree or Title Awarded
Architectural Drafting & Engineering Technology*	6	*Tgo. Delineante de Arquitectura e Ingeniería*
Bacteriology & Clinical Laboratory	8	*Bacteriólogo y Laboratorista Clínico*
Chemical Engineering	10	*Ing. Químico*
Chemistry	10	*Químico*
Civil Engineering	10	*Ing. Civil*
Education:		
Biology	10	*Lic. en Biología*
Chemistry	10	*Lic. en Química*
Design§	3	*Lic. en Dibujo*
Electromechanics§	3	*Lic. en Electromecánica*

Electronics§	3	*Lic. en Electrónica*
Languages	10	*Lic. en Idiomas*
Mathematics	10	*Lic. en Matemáticas*
Physics	10	*Lic. en Física*
Topography & Construction§	3	*Lic. en Topografía y Construcción*
Electrical Engineering	10	*Ing. Eléctrico*
Industrial Engineering	10	*Ing. Industrial*
Mechanical Engineering	10	*Ing. Mecánico*
Medicine	12	*Médico*
Metallurgical Engineering	10	*Ing. Metalúrgico*
Nursing	8	*Enfermero*
Nutrition & Dietetics	8	*Nutricionista y Dietista*
Petroleum Engineering	10	*Ing. de Petróleos*
Physiotherapy	8	*Fisioterapeuta*
Social Service	8	*Servidor Social*
Systems Engineering	10	*Ing. de Sistemas*

Specialist Programs of Study. Title Awarded—*Especialista en . . . Anestesiología; Ginecología y Obstetricia; Medicina Interna; Patología.*

Master's Programs of Study. Title Awarded—*Magister en . . . Física, Ingeniería Metalúrgica; Ingeniería Química.*

Universidad Javeriana
Bogotá.
See Pontificia Universidad Javeriana, Bogotá.

Universidad La Gran Colombia
Carrera 6 No. 13-40, Bogotá.
Tel: 2344446, 2826346. Established 1951.
Enrollment: 7406. (private)

Undergraduate Programs of Study	Length	Degree or Title Awarded
Accounting, Public	10-11	*Contador Público*
Architecture	11	*Arquitecto*
Civil Engineering	12	*Ing. Civil*
Economics	10	*Economista*
Education:		
Linquistics & Literature	8-9	*Lic. en Lingüística y Literatura*
Mathematics & Physics	8	*Lic. en Matemáticas y Física*
Philosophy & History	8	*Lic. en Filosofía e Historia*
Spanish-English	8-9	*Lic. en Español-Inglés*
Spanish-French	8-9	*Lic. en Español-Francés*
Law	10-12	*Abogado*

Specialist Program of Study. Title Awarded—*Especialista en . . . Derecho Laboral.*

Seccional (Branch Campus)

Universidad La Gran Colombia-Armenia
Carrera 17 No. 22-34, Armenia.
Tel: 49795.
Enrollment: 891.

Undergraduate Programs of Study	Length	Title Awarded
Economics	10	*Economista*
Law	10-11	*Abogado*

Universidad Libre.
See Corporación Universidad Libre de Colombia.

Universidad Nacional de Colombia (UNC)
Ciudad Universitaria, Bogota.
Tel: 2699111, 2691700, 2691411. Established 1826.
Enrollment: 18,470. (public/national)

Undergraduate Programs of Study	Length	Degree or Title Awarded
Accounting, Public	10	*Contador Público*
Agricultural Engineering	10	*Ing. Agrícola*
Agronomy	10	*Ing. Agrónomo*
Animal Science	10	*Zootecnista*
Anthropology	8	*Lic. en Antropología*
Architecture	10	*Arquitecto*
Band Direction	8	*Director de Banda*
Biology	10	*Biólogo*
Business Administration	10	*Administrador de Empresas*
Ceramics	10	*Maestro en Ceramica*
Chemical Engineering	10	*Ing. Químico*
Chemistry	10	*Químico*
Choral & Wind Instruments	8	*Lic. en Cuerdas y Viento*
Choral Direction	8	*Director de Coros*
Civil Engineering	10	*Ing. Civil*
Dentistry	9	*Dr. en Odontología*
Economics	10	*Economista*
Education:		
Biology	8	*Lic. en Biología*
Chemistry	8	*Lic. en Química*
Mathematics	8	*Lic. en Matemáticas*
Pedagogy & Educational Administration	8	*Lic. en Pedagogía y Administración Educativa*
Physics	8	*Lic. en Física*
Social Studies	8	*Lic. en Sociales*
Electrical Engineering	10	*Ing. Electricista*
English & French	8	*Lic. en Filología e Idiomas— Especialidad en . . .*
English or French & Classical Languages	8	*Lic. en Filología y Idiomas— Especialidad en . . .*

Engraving	10	Maestro en Bellas Artes— Especialidad Grabado
Ethnomusicology	8	Lic. en Etnomusicología
Geology	10	Geólogo
Graphic Design	8	Lic. en Diseño Gráfico
Industrial Design	10	Diseñador Industrial
Law	10	Abogado
Mathematics	10	Matemático
Mechanical Engineering	10	Ing. Mecánico
Medicine	12	Dr. en Medicina
Musical Composition	12	Maestro en Composición Musical
Music Teaching	8	Lic. en Pedagogía Musical
Nursing	8	Enfermero
Nutrition & Dietetics	8	Lic. en Nutrición y Dietética
Occupational Therapy	7	Lic. en Terapia Ocupacional
Orchestra Direction	10	Director de Orquesta
Organ	8	Lic. en Organo
Painting	10	Maestro en Bellas Artes— Especialidad Pintura
Percussion	8	Lic. en Percusión
Pharmacy	10	Químico Farmacéutico
Philosophy	8	Lic. en Filosofía
Physical Therapy	7	Lic. en Terapia Física
Physics	10	Físico
Piano	8	Lic. en Piano
Psychology	10	Psicólogo
Sculpture	10	Maestro en Bellas Artes— Especialidad Escultura
Singing	8	Lic. en Canto
Social Work	8	Lic. en Trabajo Social
Sociology	8	Lic. en Sociología
Spanish & Classical Languages	8	Lic. en Filología e Idiomas— Especialidad en . . .
Spanish & French or English	8	Lic. en Filología e Idiomas— Especialidad en . . .
Speech Therapy	7	Lic. en Terapia del Lenguaje
Statistics	10	Estadístico
Systems Engineering	10	Ing. de Sistemas
Veterinary Medicine	10	Dr. en Medicina y Veterinaria

Specialist Programs of Study. Title Awarded—*Especialista en* . . . *Anestesiología; Ciencias Penales y Penitenciarias; Cirugía General; Cirugía Plástica; Derecho Laboral y Seguridad Social; Dermatología; Enfermería Cardiorespiratoría y Renal; Enfermería en Salud Mental; Estomatología Pediátrica; Ginecología y Obstetricia; Medicina Interna; Neurocirugía; Neurología; Oftalmología; Ortodoncia; Ortopedia; Otorrinolaringología; Patología; Patología Infecciosa; Pediatría; Psiquiatría; Radiología; Rehabilitación; Reumatología; Urología.*

Master's Programs of Study. Title Awarded—*Magister en* . . . *Administración en Enfermería; Biología Marina; Botánica y Fisiología Vegetal; Ciencias Agrarias (ICA-UN "PEC"); Desarrollo Rural; Economía; Educación en Enfermería; Entomología; Estadística; Farmacología; Filosofía; Física; Fitopatología; Genética Humana; Genética y Mejoramiento; Ingeniería Civil—Ambiental, Estructuras, Geotecnia, Hidráulica, Sanitaria, Transportes y Vías;*

Ingeniería de Sistemas; Ingeniería Eléctrica—Potencia Eléctrica; Matemáticas; Medicina Veterinaria Preventiva; Microbiología; Nutrición Animal; Patología Animal; Periodoncia; Producción Agrícola; Producción Animal; Química; Sistemática (Botánica y Zoología), Suelos.

Seccionales (Branches Campuses)

Universidad Nacional de Colombia-Manizales
Carrera 27 No. 64-60, Apartado Aéreo 127, Manizales.
Tel: 54189, 54190.
Enrollment: 2193.

Undergraduate Programs of Study	Length	Title Awarded
Architecture	11	*Arquitecto*
Business Administration	10	*Administrador de Empresas*
Chemical Engineering	10	*Ing. Químico*
Civil Engineering	10	*Ing. Civil*
Electrical Engineering	10	*Ing. Eléctrico*
Industrial Engineering	10	*Ing. Industrial*

Universidad Nacional de Colombia-Medellín
Autopista Robledo Carretera al Mar, Medellín.
Tel: 300540, 300111.
Enrollment: 4814.

Undergraduate Programs of Study	Length	Degree or Title Awarded
Administrative Engineering	10	*Ing. Administrador*
Agricultural Economics	10	*Economista Agrícola*
Agricultural Engineering	10	*Ing. Agrícola*
Agronomy	10	*Ing. Agrónomo*
Animal Science	10	*Zootecnista*
Architecture	11	*Arquitecto*
Arts	8	*Lic. en Artes*
Building Construction	11	*Arquitecto Constructor de Edificios*
Chemical Engineering	10	*Ing. Químico*
Civil Engineering	11	*Ing. Civil*
Electrical Engineering	10	*Ing. Electricista*
Forestry Engineering	10	*Ing. Forestal*
Forestry Technology*	6	*Tgo. Forestal*
Geological Engineering	10	*Ing. Geólogo*
History	10	*Historiador*
Industrial Engineering	10	*Ing. Industrial*
Mathematics	10	*Matemático*
Mechanical Engineering	10	*Ing. Mecánico*
Mining & Metallurgical Engineering	10	*Ing. de Minas y Metalurgia*

Petroleum Engineering   10   *Ing. de Petróleos*

Master's Programs of Study. Title Awarded—*Magister en . . . Ingeniería Sanitaria; Matemáticas; Planificación Física Urbana.*

Universidad Nacional de Colombia-Palmira
Carrera 32, Palmira.
Enrollment: 879.

Undergraduate Programs of Study	Length	Title Awarded
Agricultural Engineering	10	*Ing. Agrícola*
Agronomy	10	*Ing. Agrónomo*
Animal Science	10	*Zootecnista*

Universidad Pedagógica Nacional
Calle 72 No. 11-86, Apartado Aéreo 53040, Bogotá.
Tel: 2352488, 2492853. Established 1955.
Enrollment: 4415. (public/national)

Undergraduate Programs of Study	Length	Degree Awarded
Education:		
Biology	8	*Lic. en Biología*
Biology & Chemistry	8	*Lic. en Biología y Química*
Chemistry	8	*Lic. en Química*
Educational Administration	8	*Lic. en Administración Educativa*
Electricity	8	*Lic. en Electricidad*
Electronics	8	*Lic. en Electrónica*
English	8	*Lic. en Inglés*
French	8	*Lic. en. Francés*
Geography	8	*Lic. en Geografía*
Gymnastics	8	*Lic. en Gimnasia*
History	8	*Lic. en Historia*
Mathematics	8	*Lic. en Matemáticas*
Mathematics & Physics	8	*Lic. en Matemáticas y Física*
Mechanics	8	*Lic. en Mecánica*
Philosophy	8	*Lic. en Filosofía*
Physical Education	8	*Lic. en Educación Física*
Physics	8	*Lic. en Física*
Preschool Education	8	*Lic. en Educación Pre-escolar*
Psychology & Pedagogy	8	*Lic. en Psicología y Pedagogía*
Recreation	8	*Lic. en Recreación*
Social Sciences	8	*Lic. en Ciencias Sociales*
Socioeconomics	8	*Lic. en Socio-Economía*
Spanish	8	*Lic. en Español*
Spanish & Languages	8	*Lic. en Español y Lenguas*
Sports	8	*Lic. en Deportes*
Teaching Music	8	*Lic. en Pedagogía Musical*

Technical Drawing   8   *Lic. en Dibujo Técnico*

Master's Programs of Study. Title Awarded—*Magister en Educación con especialidad en . . . Administración Educativa; Docencia; Física; Investigación Educativa y Análisis Curricular; Investigación Socio-Educativa; Matemáticas; Orientación y Asesoría Escolar; Salud.*

Universidad Pedagógica y Tecnológica de Colombia
Carretera Central del Norte, Tunja.
Tel: 2173-77. Established 1953.
Enrollment: 5086. (public/national)

Undergraduate Programs of Study	Length	Degree or Title Awarded
Agricultural Engineering	10	*Ing. Agrónomo*
Business Administration	9-11	*Administrador de Empresas*
Economics	9-11	*Economista*
Education:		
Biology & Chemistry	8	*Lic. en Biología y Química*
Chemistry & Biology	8	*Lic. en Química y Biología*
Educational Psychology	8	*Lic. en Psicopedagogía*
Mathematics & Physics	8	*Lic. en Matemáticas y Física*
Modern Languages & Spanish	8	*Lic. en Idiomas Modernos y Español*
Physical Education	8	*Lic. en Educación Física*
Physics & Mathematics	8	*Lic. en Física y Matemáticas*
Preschool Education	8	*Lic. en Educación Pre-escolar*
Social Studies	8-11	*Lic. en Ciencias Sociales*
Spanish Philology & French or English	8	*Lic. en Filología Española y Francés o Inglés*
Electromechanical Engineering	10	NA
Metallurgical Engineering	10	*Ing. Metalúrgico*
Nursing	8	*Enfermero*
Transport & Road Engineering	10	*Ing. de Transportes y Vías*

Master's Programs of Study. Title Awarded—*Magister en . . . Historia; Orientación y Consejería Escolar.*

Seccionales (Branch Campuses)

Universidad Pedagógica y Tecnológica de Colombia-Chinquinquirá.
Calle 18 No. 10-37, Chiquinquirá.
Tel: 598.
Enrollment: 163.
No further information available.

Universidad Pedagógica y Tecnológica de Colombia-Duitama
Carrera 18 Calle 23, Duitama.
Tel: 2181, 2889.
Enrollment: 270.

Undergraduate Programs of Study	Length	Degree Awarded
Agricultural Administration	10	NA
Education:		
Industrial Education	11	*Lic. en Educación Industrial*
Mathematics & Statistics	8	NA
Electromechanical Engineering	10	NA
Hotel & Tourism Administration	10	NA
Industrial Administration	10	NA

Universidad Pedagógica y Tecnológica de Colombia-Sogamoso
Calle 11 No. 10-61, Sogamoso.
Tel: 3077, 3670.
Enrollment: 505.

Undergraduate Programs of Study	Length	Title Awarded
Accounting, Public	10	*Contador Público*
Geological Engineering	10	NA
Industrial Engineering	10	NA
Mining Engineering	10	*Ing. de Minas*

Universidad Pontificia Bolivariana
Calle 52, No. 40-88, Apartado Aéreo 1178, Medellín.
Tel: 497199 Conm. 430300. Established 1936.
Enrollment: 4605. (private)

Undergraduate Programs of Study	Length	Degree or Title Awarded
Architecture & Urban Planning	10	*Arquitecto y Urbanista*
Business Administration	6	*Tgo. en Administración de*
Technology*		*Empresas*
Chemical Engineering	10	*Ing. Químico*
Education:		
Education & Religious Studies	8	*Lic. en Educación y Ciencias*
		Religiosas
Languages	8	*Lic. en Idiomas*
Mathematics & Physics	8	*Lic. en Matemáticas y Física*
Mathematics & Statistics	8	*Lic. en Matemáticas y Estadística*
Social Sciences	8	*Lic. en Ciencias Sociales*
Electrical Engineering	10	*Ing. Eléctrico*
Electronic Engineering	10	*Ing. Electrónico*
Graphic Design	10	*Diseñador Gráfico*
Industrial Design	10	*Diseñador Industrial*
Law	10	*Abogado*

Mechanical Engineering	10	*Ing. Mecánico*
Medicine	11	*Medico*
Philosophy & Letters	8	*Diplomado en Filosofía y Letras*
Social Communication	8	*Comunicador Social*
Social Work	8	*Trabajador Social*
Sociology	8	*Sociólogo*
Theology	12	*Teólogo*

Specialist Programs of Study. Title Awarded—*Especialista en . . . Anestesiología, Reanimación y Cuidado Intensivo; Derecho Civil-Comercial; Derecho Laboral; Derecho Público; Medicina Interna; Ortopedia y Traumatología.*

Universidad Popular del Cesar
Calle 16 No. 4-100, Apartado Aéreo 590, Valledupar.
Tel: 3293, 4144, 2296.
Enrollment: 584. (public/national)

Undergraduate Programs of Study	Length	Degree or Title Awarded
Accounting, Public	10	*Contador Público*
Business Administration	10	*Administrador de Empresas*
Education: Mathematics & Physics	8	*Lic. en Matemáticas y Física*

Universidad Santiago de Cali
Carrera 5 No. 7-25, Apartado Aéreo 4102, Cali.
Tel: 701261, 891693. Established 1958.
Enrollment: 5455. (private)

Undergraduate Programs of Study	Length	Degree or Title Awarded
Accounting, Public	10	*Contador Público*
Business Administration	10	*Administrador de Empresas*
Education:		
Biology & Chemistry	10	*Lic. en Biología y Química*
Languages & Literature	9	*Lic. en Literatura e Idiomas*
Mathematics	9	*Lic. en Matemáticas*
Social Sciences	9	*Lic. en Ciencias Sociales*
Law	10	*Abogado*

Master's Programs of Study. Title Awarded—*Magister en . . . Criminología, Ciencias Penales y Penitenciarias.*

Universidad Santo Tomás
Bogotá.
See Universidad de Santo Tomás, Bogotá.

Universidad Social Católica de La Salle
Calle 11 No. 1-47, Bogotá.
Tel: 2346137, 2830900, 2825696. Established 1964.
Enrollment: 7357. (private)

Undergraduate Programs of Study	Length	Degree or Title Awarded
Accounting, Public	10	*Contador Público*
Agricultural Administration Technology*	6	*Tgo. en Administración Agropecuaria*
Animal Science	10	NA
Architecture	10	*Arquitecto*
Business Administration	10	*Administrador de Empresas*
Civil Engineering	10	*Ing. Civil*
Economics	10	*Economista*
Education:		
Chemistry & Biology	8	*Lic. en Química y Biología*
Mathematics & Physics	8	*Lic. en Matemáticas y Física*
Modern Languages	8	*Lic. en Lenguas Modernas*
Religious Studies	8	*Lic. en Estudios Religiosos*
Library Science	8	*Bibliotecólogo y Archivista*
Optometry	10	*Optómetra*
Philosophy & Letters	8	*Profesional en Filosofía y Letras*
Social Work	8	*Trabajador Social*
Statistics	9	*Estadístico*
Veterinary Medicine	10	NA

Master's Programs of Study. Title Awarded—*Magister en . . . Administración de Empresas; Docencia Universitaria; Filosofía y Letras.*

Universidad Surcolombiana
Carrera 16 No. 13-20, Apartado Aéreo 192, Florencia.
Tel: 818, 824, 865. Established 1968.
Enrollment: 2193. (public/national)

Undergraduate Programs of Study	Length	Degree or Title Awarded
Accounting, Public	10	*Contador Público*
Animal Science	10	*Zootecnista*
Education:		
Linguistics & Literature	10	*Lic. en Lingüística y Literatura*
Mathematics & Physics	10	*Lic. en Matemáticas y Física*
Social Sciences	10	*Lic. en Ciencias Sociales*

Universidad Surcolombiana
Calle 9 No. 7-82, Apartado Aéreo 385, Neiva.
Tel: 27266, 27277. Established 1968.
Enrollment: 1950. (public/national)

Undergraduate Programs of Study	Length	Degree or Title Awarded
Accounting, Public	10	*Contador Público*

Agricultural Engineering	10	NA
Business Administration	10	Administrador de Empresas
Education:		
Educational Administration	10	Lic. en Administración Educativa
Linguistics & Literature	9	Lic. en Lingüística y Literatura
Mathematics & Physics	9	Lic. en Matemáticas y Física
Physical Education	8	Lic. en Educación Física
Nursing Technology*	6	Tgo. en Enfermería
Preschool Education Technology*	6	Tgo. en Educación Pre-escolar

Universidad Tecnológica del Chocó "Diego Luis Córdoba"
Carrera 2 No. 25-22, Apartado Aéreo 22, Quibdó.
Tel: 735, 589. Established 1968.
Enrollment: 1975. (public/national)

Undergraduate Programs of Study	Length	Degree or Title Awarded
Animal Science Technology*	7	Tgo. Agropecuario
Business Administration Technology*	7	Tgo. Administración de Empresas
Civil Works Technology*	7	Tgo. Obras Civiles
Education:		
Chemistry & Biology	9	Lic. en Química y Biología
Educational Psychology & Administration	9	Lic. en Administración y Planeamiento Educativo
Languages	9	Lic. en Idiomas
Mathematics & Physics	9	Lic. en Matemáticas y Física
Social Sciences	9	Lic. en Ciencias Sociales
Fishing Technology*	6	Tgo. Pesquero
Social Work	9	Trabajador Social

Universidad Tecnológica del Magdalena
San Pedro Alejandrino, Apartado Aéreo 731, Santa Marta.
Established 1871.
Enrollment: 1510. (public/state)

Undergraduate Programs of Study	Length	Degree or Title Awarded
Agricultural Administration Technology*	6	Tgo. en Administración Agropecuaria
Agricultural Economics	10	Economista Agrícola
Agronomy Engineering	10	Ing. Agrónomo
Education:		
Biology & Chemistry	10	Lic. en Biología y Química
Mathematics & Physics	10	Lic. en Matemáticas y Física
Social Sciences	10	Lic. en Ciencias Sociales
Fishing Engineering	10	Ing. Pesquero

Universidad Tecnológica de los Llanos Orientales
Kilómetro 11 Vía Puerto López, Apartado Aéreo 2621, Villavicencio.
Tel: 3449, 6200, 3484, 6828, 3909. Established 1974.
Enrollment: 836. (public/national)

Undergraduate Programs of Study	Length	Degree or Title Awarded
Agronomy	10	*Agrónomo*
Education:		
Agriculture	8	*Lic. en Ciencias Agropecuarias*
Mathematics & Physics	8	*Lic. en Matemáticas y Física*
Nursing Technology*	6	*Tgo. en Enfermería*
Veterinary & Animal Science	10	*Veterinario y Zootecnista*

Universidad Tecnológica de Pereira
Apartado Aéreo 97, Pereira.
Tel: 32781, 34944. Established 1958.
Enrollment: 3258. (public/national)

Undergraduate Programs of Study	Length	Degree or Title Awarded
Chemical Technology*	6	*Tgo. Químico*
Education:		
Chemical Technology§	3	*Lic. en Tecnología Química*
Electrical Technology§	3	*Lic. en Tecnología Eléctrica*
Industrial Technology§	3	*Lic. en Tecnología Industrial*
Mathematics & Physics	8	*Lic. en Matemáticas y Física*
Mechanical Technology§	3	*Lic. en Tecnología Mecánica*
Music	8	NA
Plastic Arts	8	NA
Social Sciences (History-Geography)	8	*Lic. en Ciencias Sociales (Historia-Geografía)*
Spanish & Audiovisual Communication	10	*Lic. en Español y Comunicación Audiovisual*
Electrical Engineering	10	*Ing. Electricista*
Electrical Technology*	6	*Tgo. Eléctrico*
Industrial Engineering	10	*Ing. Industrial*
Industrial Technology*	6	*Tgo. Industrial*
Mechanical Engineering	10	*Ing. Mecánico*
Mechanical Technology*	6	*Tgo. Mecánico*
Medicine	12	NA

Master's Programs of Study. Title Awarded—*Magister en . . . Administración Económica y Financiera; Investigación Operativa y Estadística.*

Appendix B

Most Recent Reforms of Colombian Secondary Education, July 17, 1978

Colombian secondary education has experienced frequent reforms during the last century. The most recent, Decree 1419 of July 17, 1978, is presented here in briefest outline. The proposed curriculums are still in a developmental stage. Only one program, the *Bachillerato en Artes* (secondary school program in the arts) has been implemented—and that as an experimental program in two schools. (See Appendix C for the arts curriculum.)

According to the Ministry of National Education, the outline given here is the complete system. Students who hold any *Bachiller* (secondary school diploma) from the new system will be eligible to enter any institution of higher education in Colombia in similar fields of study. Under the decree there will be three types of *Bachillerato* programs:

1. *Bachillerato en Artes* (arts);
2. *Bachillerato en Ciencias* (sciences);
3. *Bachillerato en Tecnología* (technology).

The *modalidades* (specializations) of each of the three *Bachillerato* programs are as follows:

• *Bachillerato en Artes*: 1) *Artes Aplicadas* (applied arts); 2) *Bellas Artes* (fine arts).

• *Bachillerato en Ciencias*: 1) *Ciencias Humanas* (humanities); 2) *Ciencias Matemáticas* (mathematical sciences); 3) *Ciencias Naturales* (natural sciences).

• *Bachillerato en Tecnología*: 1) *Agropecuaria* (general agriculture); 2) *Comercial* (commercial); 3) *Educación Física y Recreación* (physical education and recreation); 4) *Industrial* (industrial); 5) *Pedagógica* (pedagogy); 6) *Promoción de la Comunidad* (community services); 7) *Salud y Nutrición* (health and nutrition).

Appendix C

Curriculum, Experimental *Bachillerato en Artes*, (Secondary School Program in the Arts), by Grade

Subjects	Grade:	VI	VII	VIII	IX	X	XI	Total
American Geography*		—	2	—	—	—	—	2
American History*		—	2	—	—	—	—	2
Biology		—	3	3	3	—	—	9
Character		—	1	3	3	3	2	12
Chemistry		—	—	—	—	3	3	6
Classical Techniques		9	9	9	9	9	9	54
Colombian Geography		2	—	—	3	—	—	5
Colombian History		2	—	—	3	—	—	5
French		3	3	3	3	3	3	18
Grammar of Music		2	2	2	—	—	—	6
History of Art		—	—	—	—	—	1	1
History of Ballet		—	—	—	1	—	—	2
History of Dance		1	1	1	—	—	—	3
History of Music		—	—	—	—	1	1	2
Improvisation		1	—	—	—	—	—	1
Mathematics		5	5	5	5	3	3	26
National Folklore		2	2	—	—	—	—	4
Natural Science		3	—	—	—	—	—	3
Pas de Deux		—	—	—	—	2	3	5
Philosophy		—	—	—	—	3	3	6
Physics		—	—	—	—	3	3	6
Piano		1	1	1	1	1	1	6
Religion		3	3	3	2	1	1	13
Spanish		4	4	4	4	4	4	24
Theory of Folklore		—	—	—	—	1	1	2
Universal Geography		—	—	2	2	—	—	4
Universal History		—	—	2	2	—	—	4
	Total	38	38	38	41	38	38	

SOURCE: Instituto Colombiano de Ballet Clásico (Cali, February, 1983).
*History and geography of Latin America.

Appendix D

Seminary Education

Colombia's Roman Catholic seminaries fall into two broad categories: minor seminaries at the secondary school level, and major seminaries at the university level. The minor seminaries admit students directly from elementary school, and their six-year program, including the grading system, is regulated like that of any other Colombian secondary school by the Ministry of National Education. Graduates of minor seminaries receive the *Bachiller Clásico* (academic or classical secondary school diploma). Graduates of the minor seminaries may apply to study at any institution of higher education, including the major seminaries. (See Chapter Two for a description of the *Bachillerato* program leading to the *Bachiller Clásico*.)

The major seminaries are not regulated by the Ministry of National Education and therefore do not grant the *Licenciado* or any of the other degrees granted by Colombian universities. The major seminaries require a secondary school diploma (any *Bachiller*) for admission.

The seven-year program at the major seminaries is divided into two cycles. Cycle I—the first three years—is devoted to preparatory study, principally philosophy. For a curriculum of Cycle I, also known as *Ciclo Filosófico* (the philosophy cycle), see Table D.1.

Upon successful completion of Cycle I, the student is awarded a certificate that will show the grades earned. At that point, a student may decide to continue study at the seminary by entering Cycle II, a four-year program called the *Ciclo Teológico* (the theology cycle), or may transfer to other university level institutions, public or private. Transfer credits are determined by an analysis of courses.

Those who complete the second cycle usually enter the service of the church as priests. Those who are not ordained receive a certificate stating that the program was successfully completed and showing the grades received.

Table D.1. **Curriculum,** *Ciclo I, Filosófico* **(Philosophy, Cycle I) of the Major Seminaries in Colombia**

Subjects	hpw	Subjects	hpw
First Semester		Second Semester	
Christian Education I	5	Cathechism	2
History of Salvation I	3	Christian Education II	2
Intro. to Philosophy	4	Epistemology	3
Latin I	3	General Psychology	3
Methodology	2	Hist. of Ancient Philosophy	2
Music & Singing	2	Hist. of Salvation II	2
Spanish	3	Latin II	3
Total	22	Logic & Philosophy of the Language	3

Third Semester

Biblical Methodology I	3
Evaluation Psychology	3
General Sociology	2
Hist. of Medieval Philosophy	3
Latin III	3
Music & Singing	2
Natural Theology	3
Philosophical Anthropology	3
Total	22

Fifth Semester

Biblical Methodology III	3
Ethics	4
Hist. of Contemporary Philosophy	3
Latin V	3
Mass Media	2
Modern Language I	3
Theodicy & Philosophy of Religion	4
Total	22

Music & Singing	2
Total	22

Fourth Semester

Biblical Methodology II	3
Cultural Anthropology	2
Hist. of Modern Philosophy	3
Latin IV	3
Latin American Affairs	2
Metaphysics	4
Music & Singing	2
Social & Religious Psych.	3
Total	22

Sixth Semester

Biblical Methodology IV	3
Greek	3
Hist. & Philosophy of Art	2
Hist. of Latin American Philosophy	3
Mass Media	2
Modern Language II	3
Philosophy of History	2
Philosophical Synthesis	4
Total	22

SOURCE: Plan de Estudio, Colección Seminarios 1, Comisión Episcopal de Seminarios y Vocaciones, Conferencia Episcopal de Colombia, Bogotá, 1982.

Glossary

Abogado	lawyer.
agropecuaria	general agriculture including both the cultivation of crops and livestock raising.
alimentos	food.
alumno	student.
apellido	surname; family name.
aprobado	passing; approved.
archivo	file.
área	subject; area of study.
auxiliar	assistant.
Bachiller	person who has successfully completed *Bachillerato* studies; secondary school diploma.
Bachiller Académico	academic secondary school diploma.
Bachiller Agropecuario	agricultural secondary school diploma.
Bachiller en Artes	secondary school diploma in art.
Bachiller Clásico	classical secondary school diploma; considered almost identical to the academic diploma.
Bachiller Comercial	commercial secondary school diploma.
Bachiller Industrial	industrial secondary school diploma.
Bachiller Pedagógico	secondary school diploma in pedagogy.
Bachiller en Promoción Social	secondary school diploma in social studies.
Bachiller Técnico	secondary school diploma in technical studies.
Bachiller Técnico Agrícola	secondary school diploma in technical agriculture.
Bachiller Técnico Comercial	technical commercial secondary school diploma.
Bachillerato	secondary school program leading to the *Bachiller.*
bibliotecología	library science.
bien, bueno	well; good.
calificación	grade.
carrera	field of study; major; degree program.
castellano	the Spanish language.
certificado	certificate.
Ciclo Básico	basic cycle; first 4 yrs of secondary education program (yrs VI–IX).
Ciclo Filosófico	philosophy cycle of Roman Catholic major seminaries.
Ciclo Teológico	theology cycle of Roman Catholic major seminaries.

Ciclo Vocacional	advanced secondary cycle under new system; "vocational" denotes career choice, not lower technical education.
Cirujano	surgeon.
ciudadano	citizen; used as form of address.
colegio	generally a private secondary school; may also be a postsecondary institution.
comercio exterior	international trade.
contaduría	accounting.
curso	course.
decreto	decree.
deporte	sports.
derecho	right; law.
desarrollo	development.
dibujo	drawing; drafting.
diseño	design.
Doctor	holder of *doctor* degree.
educación media	refers to all types of post-elementary education, usually yrs VI–XI.
egresado	colloquial title for students who complete required coursework, but not the thesis and/or comprehensive exams, and thus have not been awarded the *Licenciado*; this title has no legal or official significance in Colombia.
El Examen de Estado	national university entrance examination.
empresa	business; enterprise.
enfermería	nursing.
enseñanza	teaching.
escuela	school.
escuelas vocacionales agrícolas	vocational agricultural schools.
Especialista	specialist; title given for graduate-level program of specialization.
examen de grado	oral defense of thesis required for graduate degrees (*Magister, Doctor*).
examen de habilitación	make-up examination.
excelente	excellent.
Experto	at secondary level, a diploma or title granted under the pre-1974 system at end of first cycle (9 yrs of education) of the industrial *Bachillerato* program; at postsecondary level, a 2-yr diploma program offered prior to 1980.
Exención de Matrícula	tuition waiver.
facultad	basic division of traditional Colombian university; college or school within a university.
fecha	date.
formación	level of academic studies; training.

Formación Avanzada o de Postgrado	graduate study; Level 4 of higher education studies under Decree 80.
Formación Intermedia Profesional	intermediate professional studies; Level 1 of higher education studies under Decree 80.
Formación Tecnológica	technological studies; Level 2 of higher education studies under Decree 80.
Formación Universitaria	University-level studies; Level 3 of higher education studies under Decree 80.
idioma	language.
instituto	institute; common term for educational institutions at all levels.
Instituto Colombiano para el Fomento de la Educación Superior (ICFES)	Colombian Institute for the Promotion of Higher Education.
Institutos Nacionales de Educación Media Diversificada (INEM)	comprehensive secondary schools.
intensidad horaria	hours per week.
jardín infantil	kindergarten.
Licenciado	first university degree; holder of such a degree.
Licenciatura	basic full-length undergraduate program.
liceo	term used to designate a secondary school, generally private.
Maestro, Maestro Superior, Normalista Superior	teacher; pre-1974 diploma awarded for completion of secondary education in a normal (teacher training) school.
Magister, Magister Scientiae, Maestría, or Master	master's degree.
malo	bad; poor; in some grading systems a failing grade.
Matrícula de Honor	honor scholarship.
Médico	medical doctor.
muy bien	very good.
muy mal	very bad; poor.
nacimiento	birth.
niño	child.
nombre	name, first name, given name.
nota	grade, mark.
odontología	dentistry.
Perito	title awarded for completion of 2- to 4-semester program offered at postsecondary level prior to 1980.
pésimo	terrible.
promedio	grade average.
promedio general de calificaciones	overall grade average.
promedio número	final grade average.
pruebas de los exámenes de estado	national entrance examinations.

química	chemistry.
regular	average, satisfactory.
Secretario de Educación	secretary of education.
Servicio Nacional de Aprendizaje (SENA)	National Apprenticeship Service.
Servicio Nacional de Pruebas	National Testing Service.
Técnico	technical; technician; 6- to 7-semester program offered at postsecondary level prior to 1980.
Técnico Profesional Intermedio (TPI)	intermediate professional technician.
Tecnólogo	technologist.
Tecnólogo Especializado	specialized technologist (program leading to this title not yet approved by ICFES at time of publication of this volume).
tesis de grado	thesis.
Título	title or diploma; a generic term used at all education levels.
trabajo de grado	thesis.
Unidades de Labor Académica (ULAs)	"units of academic work"; under Decree 80, the official unit of measure for coursework completed at postsecondary level.
zootecnia	animal science.

Useful References

Although a great deal of information about Colombian education exists, most of it is in Spanish and is difficult to obtain. The information available in English is either out of date or of limited use to interested persons. The following selected list includes publications that will be most helpful to admissions officers.

A. Works Available in English

Low-Maus, Rodolfo. *Compendium of the Colombian Educational System*. Bogotá: Editorial Andes, 1971.

Renner, Richard R. *Education for a New Colombia*. Washington, D.C.: U.S. Government Printing Office, 1971.

Wellington, Stanley. "Educational Reform and Innovation: A Study of the New Comprehensive Secondary School in Cali, Colombia." Ph.D. dissertation, University of Illinois, 1976.

B. Works Available Only in Spanish

Bohórquez-Casallas, Luis Antonio. *La Evolución Educativa en Colombia*. Bogotá: Cultural Colombiana, LTDA, 1956.

Guerra, Luis Alejandro. *Legislación Escolar Colombiana*. 2a ed. Bogotá: Voluntad, 1971.

Instituto Colombiano para el Fomento de la Educación Superior. *Directorio de la Educación Superior en Colombia, 1981*. División de Recursos Bibliográficos. Bogotá, D.E.: División de Publicaciones del ICFES, 1981.

Instituto Colombiano para el Fomento de la Educación Superior, (ed.). *Reforma de la Educación Post-Secundaria: Compilación Legislativa*. 2a ed. Bogotá: División de Publicaciones del ICFES, 1982.

Ministerio de Educación Nacional. *Institutos Nacionales de Educación Media Serie Divulgativa 2*. Bogotá: Publicación de la Sección de Documentación y Difusión del ICCE, 1970.

Muñoz-Delgado, Juan Jacobo. "La Reforma de la Educación Media, Decreto 080 de 1974." Bogotá: Ministerio de Educación Nacional, 1974. (Mimeographed)

Index

NATIONAL COUNCIL ON THE EVALUATION OF FOREIGN EDUCATIONAL CREDENTIALS

The Council is an interassociational group that serves as a forum for developing consensus on the evaluation and recognition of certificates, diplomas, and degrees awarded throughout the world. It also assists in establishing priorities for research and publication of country, regional, or topical studies. One of its main purposes is to review and modify admissions and placement recommendations drafted by World Education Series authors or others who might ask for such review. (The practices followed in fulfilling this purpose are explained on page 64.)

Chairperson—Gary Hoover, Director, Foreign Student Admissions, University of the Pacific, Stockton, CA 95211.

Vice Chairperson/Secretary—Karlene Dickey, Associate Dean of Graduate Studies and Research, Stanford University, Stanford, CA 94305.

MEMBER ORGANIZATIONS AND THEIR REPRESENTATIVES: American Association of Collegiate Registrars and Admissions Officers—Chairperson of World Education Series Committee, Alan Margolis, Registrar, Queens College, City University of New York, Flushing, NY 11367; G. James Haas, Associate Director of Admissions, Indiana University, Bloomington, IN 47405; Kitty Villa, Acting Assistant Director, International Office, The University of Texas at Austin, Austin, TX 78712. American Association of Community and Junior Colleges—Philip J. Gannon, President, Lansing Community College, Lansing, MI 48901. American Council on Education—Joan Schwartz, Senior Program Associate, Office on Educational Credit and Credentials, American Council on Education, Washington, DC 20036. College Entrance Examination Board—Sanford C. Jameson, Director, Office of International Education, College Entrance Examination Board, Washington, DC 20036. Council of Graduate Schools—Andrew J. Hein, Assistant Dean, The Graduate School, University of Minnesota-Twin Cities, Minneapolis, MN 55455. Institute of International Education—Martha Renaud, Manager, Placement Services Division, Institute of International Education, New York, NY 10017. National Association for Foreign Student Affairs—James Frey, Executive Director, Educational Credential Evaluators, Inc., Milwaukee, WI 53217; David Horner, Director, Office of International Students and Scholars, Michigan State University, E. Lansing, MI 48824-1035; Joann Stedman, Director, Office of International Student Services, Columbia University, New York, NY 10027.

OBSERVER ORGANIZATIONS AND THEIR REPRESENTATIVES:
USIA—Joseph Bruns, Chief, Student Support Services Division, Office of Academic Programs, USIA, Washington, DC 20547.
AID—Hattie Jarmon, Education Specialist, Office of International Training, U.S. Department of State/AID, Washington, DC 20523.
USOE—Robert Barendsen, Specialist on Education in Far Eastern Countries, U.S. Department of Education, Washington, DC 20202.
State of New York Education Department—Mary Jane Ewart, Associate in Comparative Education, State Education Department, The University of the State of New York, Albany, NY 12230.